Comments from Respected Reviewers

"Carol Casale has beautifully shared simple and yet profound lessons she has learned from her little dog, Cassy. The deep Love and Heart of God, Himself, permeates every chapter. I, personally, was drawn to *Paws for Praise*. May all who read Carol and little Cassy's story be drawn into an ever-deepening relationship with Jesus Christ."

-Marilyn Couch

"A delightful array of vignettes, featuring Cassy the puppy, that give the reader a glimpse of God's profound love for His most treasured creatures—us!"

-William J. Vanarthos, M.D.
Author: "What are the Odds?: Are you willing to gamble with your eternity?"

"*Paws for Praise* is a heartfelt tale depicting the special relationship between a dog and its master. The author does a great job of drawing a parallel connecting God's love for His children and the special bond between a pet and its loving owner. *Paws for Praise* sweetly honors the One who created both Cassy and her loving master."

-Stacy Childs

More Comments from Respected Reviewers

"A few years back I heard an agnostic ridiculing God. Her comment was 'Ha, God is dog spelt backwards.' Little did she realize that God always knows exactly what He is doing even down to naming all his creations. Who else besides God loves us unconditionally, is always willing to forgive us, wants to hear us call His name and never tires of being part of our lives—our furry companions that's who. *Paws for Praise* is such a sweet read. The author's love for God (and her dog) is quite evident. . . No matter what life throws at us, we can always be comforted sitting at our Master's feet just as our pets are comforted sitting by us."

-Priscilla Hoffman

"I didn't think I would ever be '*That* Person' as the author says, or, '*That* dog lover,' but after reading these charming tales, it is hard not to fall in love—with the book, and with Cassy!"

-Greg McElveen
Publisher, Ghost Writer

"Who knew that a dog could teach us so much about God's word? I intend to give all my dog parent clients a copy. Scripture is perfectly placed within each heartwarming story."

-Stephanie Silk
Dog walker, sitter, with numerous clients and happy dogs!

Paws for Praise

*Lessons learned from our dog about
a relationship with God*

Carol Casale

Copyright Page

Author: Carol Casale
Editor: Greg McElveen
Cover Design: Carol Casale, Olivia Vanarthos
Illustrations, Photos: Copyright © 2017 Carol and Joe Casale

All Scripture verses are taken from the New International Version (NIV 2011) of the Bible unless otherwise specified.

Library of Congress Control Number: 2017953345
Library of Congress subject headings:
1. BR115 Christianity in relation to special subjects
2. GR700-860 Folklore - Animals, plants, and minerals

BIASC Classification Suggestions:
1. REL012020 RELIGION / Christian Life / Devotional
2. PET010000 PETS / Essays & Narratives
3. REL012040 RELIGION / Christian Life / Inspirational
4. PET004000 PETS / Dogs / General
5. PET000000 PETS / General

Paperback ISBN-13:   978-1-937355-41-8
eBook ISBN-13:   978-1-937355-42-5

Published by Big Mac Publishers
www.bigmacpublishers.com / Kingston, TN 37763
Written and processed in the United States of America

Table of Contents

Preface

My life BC (before Cassy) had been as busy and active as life gets when you are a full-time working mom while juggling three children at home. Although our children were well past the young childhood years when I returned to nursing, anyone who knows me understands that the position I held as "MOM and CEO" of the home was always first and foremost in my life. Many questioned why I would then bring a puppy into an already hectic life.

Let me bring you back to 2007 when the decision to take in a pup was made. During this time, I was happily working alongside several Mohs skin surgeons, often assisting with the removal of devastating skin cancers and subsequent facial reconstruction. One of the physicians, Dr. Greg Viehman, was confident, skilled and an admired surgeon, who was typically upbeat and personable. However, on one particular day, I noticed he had a saddened face and downcast spirit. As I approached his office to review a patient's case with him, I stopped dead in my tracks just outside his door. He was clearly overwhelmed with emotion and upset. He shared with me that his dog of many years was getting to the end of her life and probably wouldn't make it through the week. I didn't know what to say! His look of grief moved my heart.

Soon after, I began to question how a grown man, with a beautiful family and successful career could be so distraught over a dog. Perhaps I needed to consider getting a dog to love. After all, the nest was beginning to empty with the pending wedding of our daughter, and middle son living away from home while attending college. Little did I know that bringing a pup into our lives would change me so dramatically. Who would have thought that I would become *That Person*, you know, the one who is crazy about their dog. Indeed; Cassy has altered life in the Casale home, but we are all so grateful for her. We love our scruffy girl and will continue to love and care for her, especially now as she is entering her senior years.

Introduction

1 Corinthians 13:4 says, "Love is patient, love is kind. It does not envy, it does not boast, it is not proud."

Is it possible to make the claim that the love relationship between dog and master can be compared to the love relationship between people and God? I believe this to be true and it was this very sentiment that led me to write this little book of doggie tales. I hope you, as the reader will share my thoughts on this, yet understand that in no way am I minimizing the ultimate expression of love toward us that was made through the sacrifice of Jesus' life, death, and resurrection.

The parallels I outline are merely examples of how natural it is for a dog to love their master. A dog's love of course, pales to the Agape love of the Father; however, I do see the unconditional love of God mirrored by Cassy and other dogs I have come to know. In turn, I hope these snapshots inspire love for our Master, God and Father in Heaven, who loves us unconditionally.

My goal in sharing these stories, which occurred during the past decade, is to share this incredible and sweet love expressed by her to me with all of you. So, enjoy. I hope you find them *pawfectly* entertaining.

Author Carol Casale, (a.k.a. "CC")
with Cassy and Grandchild

Dedication

This is the only book I have ever written or have even thought of writing; therefore, I would like to thank the Lord Jesus for giving me the inspiration to decode my budding love for an animal into the precious words penned in this little book of tales. I especially want to thank my husband Joe; a friend and constant supporter, who shares my love for Cassy.

This book is dedicated as well to our three children who have come to understand that their mother has not lost her mind, but is just sharing the love in her heart for our precious four-pawed pet.

I want to thank all my friends who supported me, but especially the following; Dr. Bill Vanarthos, Stacy and Don Childs, and Dr. Greg Viehman who collectively encouraged me to assemble these stories into a book.

Last, but certainly not least, I could not have learned these lessons (that I now cherish deeply) about the relationship between dog and master if it were not for Cassy. She will always live in my heart.

Paws for Praise

Chapter 1

Day One

After being married for almost 27 years and raising three children, I thought it was about time to get a puppy. All I had to do was convince my husband Joe! Now, Joe loves hot dogs, especially with mustard and sauerkraut, but real, live, eating, pooping, barking dogs is another story. I really had my work cut out for me. Joe always wants to please me, but convincing him that we should be pet parents wouldn't be easy. Just getting him to come with me for a look at the pups was something that I had to carefully plan out. After all, was bringing a dog into our lives a good decision? Was I using my head or my heart to decide? Joe is so logical whereas I'm the sensitive motherly type. Could it be that I am lamenting over becoming an empty nester?

I didn't want the decision to bring a dog into our home to be solely mine, so I waited to broach the subject with Joe at just the right moment. Before we retired that night, I brought up the topic again.

My heart pounded in my throat as I organized my words. "Well, what do you think? Can we get a puppy?" A faint smile outlined his lips. He looked right at me and said, "How about if we go and take a look and then decide. Sound like a plan?"

After Joe graciously agreed to go look at the pups, we scheduled a visit for the following Sunday. As you can imagine, the next four days seemed eternally long. Like an overanxious child waiting for the big day to arrive, that day couldn't come quickly enough.

At 2:00 p.m. on that following Sunday afternoon, we anxiously walked into a room of squealing newborn puppies. We both felt nervous, like first-time parents. Should we really do this? After all, we had raised three children, but do we know how to raise a puppy? What if we get home and change our minds, or suppose our puppy gets sick or hurt? Will I know what to do? Who do I call, where do I go? AAH! Should I leave right now and go back to our dog-free life? After all, it's been fine just the way it's always been. Right?

"Wait! Look at that little one over there?" I said, frantically pointing at the sweetest little champagne-colored pup. Joe's eyes followed my lead. As I bent down on both knees and gently scooped her up into my jittery hands, I thought, *is this the long-awaited pup that would capture our hearts and become our new little family member?* I glanced over and saw a wide grin on Joe's face. He had the look of a proud new papa. I gently placed the pup into his calm loving hands. Why am I so nervous? Then the doubts began; *Do I have what it takes to meet all the needs of a new puppy? Should we turn around and go home empty-handed hoping someone else might choose to give this playful precious pup a forever home? No! This feels as right as rain.* Joe and I had found our girl.

It was her scruffy little face and brown button nose that not only put a smile on our faces, but instantly tugged at our heart strings. We both knew she was destined to be ours. We did not adopt her from a rescue center, but we did adopt her into our family. We gave her love and correction when needed. We fed and watered her and taught her how to relieve herself outside. We did all this for her because we loved her from Day One.

Did you know that God loves us from Day One? He tells us that He knit us together in our mother's womb (Psalm 139:13). Can you imagine that? He formed and shaped us into who we are today. In Jeremiah 29:11, God tells us that He has a plan for our lives, a plan for good and not evil, to bless us and to prosper us. Just knowing this comforts me. Just as Cassy was adopted into my family, God chooses to adopt us into His. I admit, it was Cassy's cute little face that really made me want her, but God doesn't choose us based on how we look or act. He chooses us to be His because He first loved us and died for us. He looks at our heart, not our outward appearance. He takes us in, cleans us up, loves us, gives us correction as needed, feeds us with His word and shows us how to cleanse ourselves of bad habits and sin through prayer and forgiveness.

1 John 1:9 says, "If we confess our sins, He is faithful and will forgive us our sins and purify us from all unrighteousness."

We had a lot of work ahead of us when we first got Cassy. Did I mention that she was our first dog? Yes, that's right, our first dog. Help!! Is anyone out there? May Day, May Day!

With lots of advice from books, friends and Cesar Milan, The Dog Whisperer, we were committed to train her and help her grow into a well- behaved doggie. Since Day One, Cassy has blessed us with love, joy and faithful companionship. There is nothing she could do that would cause us to stop loving her, abandon her or mistreat her. We love Cassy the way God loves us. He adopts us into His family for the same reason we adopt our doggies into our families. To provide a loving, secure environment. Our Master desires that we develop trust in Him, be obedient to Him and learn to walk with Him. Isn't this what we all want from our pets? They do a great job of walking with their master. Are we as willing to walk with ours? Let's be committed to sit and stay at His feet and learn how to walk with our eyes on Him.

Chapter 1: Day One

Chapter 2

The Chew Stage

The first few weeks as pet parents were definitely life-altering. Notice I said life-altering and not life-changing. Becoming parents to our three children was indeed life-changing. Bringing Cassy into our home altered our routine for several months, but slowly we got accustomed to having a pet.

In the early weeks of her training, we needed to provide her with lots of chew toys and bully sticks. If we hadn't, she would have soothed her tender gums and growing teeth on my furniture, shoes, and baseboards. She wasn't a bad puppy; she was just a puppy and puppies chew—A LOT! Thankfully, she never destroyed anything in our house. Although we worked hard to prevent chew accidents, there was one encounter on which Joe and I now look back on and laugh.

One evening while we were eating our dinner, we wondered where Cassy was. It was a typical midweek evening after a busy workday. We finally sat down to eat, relax, and enjoy good food and conversation. Cassy is usually underfoot with one of us or at least within several yards of where we are, but not this night. She was unseen and unheard. This should have been the first red flag. Joe called her name, "Cassy, Cass, come here girl." Out she came from our bedroom. "Good girl" he said as he petted her lovingly on her head.

A few minutes later, she was again nowhere in sight. Joe lifted his voice a little louder and said, "Cassy, come." Out she came, this time her tail was wagging with excitement, and she had a real bounce in her step. "Good girl," he said and even rewarded her with a treat for her quick obedient response to her master's call. She quickly disappeared again after munching her crunchy puppy biscuit.

I suddenly thought, *I better see what she is up to.*

I meandered into my bedroom hoping to see my puppy girl curled up with her special doggy blanket. She was in my bedroom alright, but she was not curled up sleeping. Cassy was having a good time chewing a pillow sham that she had been able to pull onto the floor from my bed. And to top it off, we had been unwittingly telling her, "good girl" and rewarding her with treats. She must have thought, *this is great; I get to chew the pillow and get rewarded for chewing it!*

God desires to reward us just like we want to reward our dogs. He thankfully, chooses to reward us solely by His grace and not based on what we deserve. If He rewarded us based solely on our good deeds, none of us would ever receive His reward. God desires also to keep us from situations that could cause us harm or take us in the opposite direction of where He knows we should be going. He trains us through His word for successful living. He shapes us with love, gentleness, and correction when needed. He tells us to hide His word in our heart (Psalm 119:11). If we do this, He promises that we will live many years and have peace and prosperity (Proverbs 3:2).

Had I let Cassy continue chewing the pillow, she inevitably would have eaten the stuffing and would have gotten sick. Thankfully, I stopped her, not only because I liked my pillow sham, but I was concerned she might get sick. I know what is and is not good for her. My hope is that consistent discipline will keep her from getting into trouble again, keep her from harming herself, and from going in the opposite direction of where I know she should.

God knows what is and is not good for us too. He protects us by giving us His word to live by. Think of it as a Manual for Living. No matter how many times I correct Cassy for her disobedience, she still continues to love me and never holds a grudge toward me. She wants to please me all the time.

Wouldn't it be great if we always wanted to please Our Master? What if we accepted His discipline with grace and a willingness to obey, just like our four-legged friends?

Chapter 2: The Chew Stage

Chapter 3

Homecoming Everyday

We decided to *crate train* Cassy from the very beginning. Before we brought her home with us, we shopped for a crate. I wanted one that was safe and comfortable. I likewise purchased a soft lamb's-wool-type fleece blanket which I placed on the bottom of her new crate. It seemed "pawfect."

Whenever we are at home she is always in sight. She closely follows me and Joe like a shadow from room to room. She is our constant chaperone, our tag-along. Like a fly who is attracted to flypaper, her devout loyalty keeps her right underfoot. Even if she is sound asleep, like a content well fed baby, and she hears one of us leaving the room, ever so quietly, she will immediately awaken and is right on our heels. She loves being wherever we are. In the very words of Aristotle, "A friend is a single soul dwelling in two bodies." Cassy and I do not share our souls, but her faithful friendship toward me and Joe is immeasurable.

Cassy can always be found resting peacefully without a care in the world on Joe's feet while he is working at his desk. When Joe is relaxing on the couch, Cassy is right there with him, curled up on his lap like a well-protected chick under mother hen's wing. When we are getting ready to leave our home we tell her "go to your crate" and she obediently goes in it. With eyes wide open and droopy little ears, she can almost be heard saying, "OK, but I'll miss you," in a woeful agonizing way. We always give her a cookie when we go out. She looks at us sadly, but I know it is safer for her to be in a crate when no one is at home. It really is a cozy, peaceful, little place that is meant to bring her undisturbed, relaxed comfort.

When we return home, we anticipate seeing her sweet little face looking back at us. We open the crate door and watch out! She is over-the-moon happy to see us. Like the person who was just presented with a check from Publisher's Clearing House, her great fortune of having her two-favorite people return home is pure heaven sent. Whether we are gone for thirty minutes or five hours, the homecoming reception is the same. She wiggles, jumps, squeals, licks and is full of total body excitement. All we did was come home! Can you imagine if your husband, wife, kids, parents, or friends responded this way whenever you walked in the door? The sadness she may have felt when we left the house is quickly replaced with exuberance and her countenance turns to pure joy, all at the sight of seeing us return home.

Thankfully, I have never been put into a crate.

However, there are times when I do feel closed in, isolated and alone. I am sure that at various seasons of life, everyone has experienced similar feelings as these. Change for me is hard. I always want to keep things just the way they've always been. The idiom, "if it ain't broke, don't fix it," can be my life's motto. When I do get down in the dumps, I have a tendency to withdraw and isolate myself from others. It is sort of like going into my own personal crate. When I go through times of disturbed peace, I know God wants to open the crate door of my heart and set me free. "He binds up the brokenhearted and gives freedom to the captives" (Isaiah 61:1).

Have you ever felt like a *captive* to something or someone? I know I have. It is during these times of disturbed peace that I find myself shutting the door to His voice. I don't look for Him eagerly from room to room the way Cassy looks for me. Wouldn't it be wonderful if we greeted our Master with the pure joy that our dogs greet us with? When we are ready to open the door of our hearts, He is always there eager to welcome us home. "Here I am. I stand at the door [of your heart] and knock. If anyone hears my voice and opens the door, I will come in and eat with that person, and they with me" (Revelation 3:20).

Talk about a Homecoming! Just hearing these words replaces the anxiety in my heart with perfect peace. Like the calm stillness of wind-driven snow on a winter's night, my soul settles into rest. Like Cassy, my countenance turns to pure joy when I am in the presence of my Master. He promises never to leave us or forsake us (Hebrews 13:5). What is there not to be joyful about? Like our dogs, He doesn't care what we look like, how much money we have, how big our house is, or what kind of car we drive. He loves and died for us in spite of who we are— pure and simple. Can you imagine that it took the pure unconditional love of my puppy to teach me this truth?

Chapter 4

Sit, Stay, and Come

There were three basic commands I needed to teach Cassy right from the outset. Sit, Stay, and Come. As a first-time pet parent though, I was clueless; at least when it came to dog ownership. Remember I shared early on how I read dog training books and watched Cesar Milan, The Dog Whisperer? Well, we also took Cassy to Puppy Kindergarten. Her kindergarten class was specifically designed for puppies, so you can imagine how chaotic it was. There were about 12 pups of various sizes, colors, and shapes. One thing they all had in common was their awkward and playful dispositions. Yet, all three teaching sources had the same message— Sit, Stay, and Come. I soon realized that these three commands can save a pet's life if properly taught and adhered to. Imagine if danger was lurking and your precious pet ignored your command to stop and listen? The result could be life-changing or worse yet, fatal.

Cassy does great with Sit and Stay if there are no major distractions that would entice her to be defiant. For instance, when someone comes to my home to visit, she is so focused on the visitor that she can't or won't focus on my command to Sit and Stay. She wants to greet everyone that comes through the door just like she greets me when I come home; full-body wiggles, squeals, licks, jumping, grinning from ear to ear. (Well, maybe not grinning).

However, Cassy does communicate with me when she is happy, sad, frustrated, stressed, or excited. I am not alone; just ask any pet owner if their dogs communicate with them.

People primarily use verbal communication, but our pets generally rely on body language, tail wagging, shaking (particularly if frightened) as well as audible sounds like whining, howling, or barking.

When I am in the yard, and I tell Cassy to Sit and Stay, I can walk 50 feet away from her and she will not move from her sitting position. She will surrender to stillness until I say, "come Cassy, come." She will then sprint at top speed like a gazelle toward me knowing there is a "yummy, totally can't wait to eat it, scrumptious, tasty treat" in my hand.

If she happens to eye a squirrel, bunny or cat, her focus will be broken. Therein lies my challenge! It is for her benefit that she masters these commands. If she obeys my directive, telling her to Sit and Stay when a car is careening down the street that could save her life.

Telling her to Come when she is wandering too far off will keep her from potentially getting lost or hurt.

God wants us to learn to Sit, Stay, and Come also. His desire is that we, His children, master these for our own good.

He encourages us to Sit and be still. He says, "Be still and know that I am God" (Psalm 46:10). He doesn't say, "Give money, feed the poor or teach Sunday school to show that you love me." Instead, He says, "Be still."

Now don't get me wrong. Serving and giving are very important to God. He wants us to help others, to serve and love one another. It is wonderful to practice these things. But more importantly, God wants our focused love and attention.

It would be no different if you did a lot of things for your husband, wife, or kids, but never spent any quality time with them. 1 Corinthians 13:1 says, "If I speak in the tongues of men or of angels, but do not have love, I am only a resounding gong or a clanging cymbal."

God tells us to Stay. John 15:5 says, "I am the vine; you are the branches. If you remain in me and I in you, you will bear much fruit; apart from me you could do nothing." In other words, just stay connected to Him; trust Him and He will take care of you. The result will be a fruitful life of peace, joy and contentment, not confusion uncertainty and restlessness.

And the greatest blessing, is that He wants us to Come. Matthew 11:28 says, "Come to me, all of you who are weary and burdened, and I will give you rest."

Doesn't this sound refreshing? Who doesn't get weary and burdened at times? God knew we would experience times of weariness because He says He would give us rest. We wouldn't need rest if we weren't weary.

Just like Cassy, I too can get distracted and wander off down the wrong path. But, just as I lovingly but firmly re-focus her attention on me, so God does with us.

I think I will Sit (with Cassy on my lap) and Stay (I'll rub her belly) while I read His word and Come to Him with my thoughts and prayers. I feel better already. So, join me by coming to Him with your furry friend on your lap or at your feet. Our Master invites us to Come, Sit, and Stay for as long as we like

Chapter 5

Peas and Carrots

Growing up in an Italian family from Brooklyn, I understand and appreciate the passion for good food and, more importantly, the passion for eating good food. When we sat down to eat, "the breaking of bread" was just as much an emotional experience as it was a physical one. Food was intended to nourish our bodies, but it really had to taste good. After all, *love* was the secret ingredient.

Cassy gets a very balanced nutritious diet of natural, no-filler-added kibbles. She really likes her kibbles, but loves when we add peas and carrots to them. Sometimes she gets green beans, but peas and carrots really get four stars over the beans. The problem is that she will sometimes pick out the peas and carrots and leave the kibbles behind. She doesn't understand that the veggies are meant to enhance her diet, not replace it. If she only ate the veggies, she would lack the needed nutrition that her kibbles are designed to give her.

As her master, I know what her little 14-pound canine body needs to maintain good health, a shiny coat and an adequate energy level. Without adequate nutrition, she would more than likely show signs of poor health, lackluster coat, and little motivation to walk, run and play.

She would no doubt, have "dog-day afternoons and plenty of hard-day's nights."

God knows what is good and healthy for us also. He tells us to take in His word daily. It is like a satisfying meal for our spiritual nourishment. Without food, it is almost certain that we would become physically weak, anemic, malnourished, and lifeless. Without the daily bread of His word, our spiritual lives, will become weak, anemic, malnourished, and lifeless, as well.

Jesus tells us that He is the *Bread of Life* (John 6:35). He uses the illustration of food because food is vital to our well-being, just as He is vital to our well-being.

The word of God is the same today as it was yesterday and will be tomorrow. We should not pick out the parts we like and disregard the parts we don't like. We must eat the whole meal to be completely balanced and spiritually healthy. We cannot grow spiritually, if like Cassy, we pick out the peas and carrots of God's word to satisfy our own desires. God tells us in Deuteronomy 4:2, "Do not add to what I command you and do not subtract from it, but keep the commands of the Lord your God that I give you."

God is so gracious. He makes His word available to all who would desire to know Him. Every book of the Bible contains wisdom, knowledge, and insight of who our Creator is. It is like a smorgasbord of nourishing, delicious, perfectly ripe, perfectly cooked food with just the right amount of seasoning and spice. He invites everyone, old and young alike, to dine at His table daily. The Gospel is the "good news" which supplies just what we need to live and prepares us for eternity. Every part of God's word is healthy. Just like Cassy's kibbles, it is balanced nutrition with no fillers added.

So, *heavenly* dinner is served! It will not only be delicious, but will be prepared with love for all who come to the table.

Chapter 5: Peas and Carrots

Chapter 6

The Dog Who Cried Wolf

In the early months of Cassy's life, she learned some very basic commands. She was taught and mastered the Sit command and quickly responded to phrases such as, "Do you want a treat," or "would you like to go potty?"

A very effective method Joe and I used to train her when she needed to potty, was placing a bell by the door. We purchased a clerk's bell at the office supply store and taught her how to hit the bell with her paw every time we took her out to potty. She caught on very quickly, and after a few days of repeating this ritual, she learned to run to the door and "bing" it with her paw on her own. Success!

After meal time, we were consistently using this method to train her. When she finished eating, we would say to her, "do you have to go potty?" This bell-ringing method was working great! Joe and I were very happy with her progress until she figured out that the bell binging equated to going outside.

Throughout the day and evening, she would enthusiastically run to the door, bing the bell with her paw, wag her tail frantically and impatiently dance around as if to say, "Can't you hear me binging the bell? I want to go outside and play."

This was cute initially, but soon became an annoying habit. Of course, we didn't want to confuse her and ignore her attempt to alert us that she needed to go out. The bell was intended for her to tell us she needed to relieve herself, not just to go outside for playtime. Our very intuitive son Mike affectionately dubbed Cassy, "The Dog Who Cried Wolf."

This was a perfect description of our little pup. After-all, it was working.

As children of God, we may also have a tendency to cry wolf at times. When life gets busy, we can go about our day, our week or sometimes even longer without talking to the Lord. We can make decisions and choices without consulting the One who made us and knows what is best for us.

He is gracious and allows us to have this freedom, but then a day may come when we need Him because things are just not going the way we would like for them to. There are times we may cry out to Him in our hour of need, at least until our situation resolves. When our need is no longer pressing, we may be tempted to go right back to living independent of Him.

The Lord doesn't want to only hear from us when we are in crisis mode. He invites us to come to Him with all things; all the time. Jeremiah 33:3 says, "Call to Me and I will answer you and tell you great and unsearchable things you do not know."

Also, in 1 Thessalonians 5:17, we are told to pray continually.

God desires that we not only call on Him when we want something, like Cassy when she rings the bell just to go outdoors. He desires to hear from us even when all is going as it should. Being in a relationship with the Lord should prompt us to want to go to Him just like a child who goes to his or her mother or father for all things, not just when they need something.

Cassy cannot rationalize, but instead is motivated instinctively by her action- bell binging, followed by the reaction- going outside. When Cassy calls me to the door by binging the bell, I respond to her need to go outside and relieve herself. Any good, responsible, and attentive pet parent would do the same.

The same is true of God. When we call on Him, He responds to us. Psalm 91:15 says, "He will call on Me, and I will answer him; I will be with him in trouble, I will rescue him and honor him."

Cassy understands, now that she is a bit older, that the bell has a purpose and is not just for entertainment. She appropriately bings when she has to relieve herself. She doesn't just bing to go out and play. She understands that the action of binging results in a reaction from me.

Once again, Cassy has learned the secret of pleasing me, her master, far better than I have. I don't want to be a kid who cries wolf; rather, I want to be the kid who cries, "Lord, Lord; thank

You for always being a prayer away. Thank You for listening, guiding and protecting me. Help me not to go my own way, but instead, acknowledge You daily, believing that You will make my path straight" (Proverbs 3:5-7).

Chapter 7

The Smudge in the Window

Eighteen months ago, BC (before Cassy), the windows in my house rarely had smudge marks on them. Now all you can see are smudge marks, especially on the glass panels on either side of my front door. Cassy's scruffy little brown-eyed face is typically peering out the window, leaving nose and tongue prints behind.

She now has figured out that different windows in the house give her different views of the outside. She might see something of interest, like a bunny, the neighbor's cat, or Tina, her friend from down the street, who moseys into our yard for a "P" stop. Cassy paces back and forth deliberately, from window to window hoping to get that "pawfect" view of whatever it is she focuses on. She will bark and squeal with delight depending on what she sees.

When I return home, and Cassy hears or sees my car nearing the house, she immediately runs upstairs and jumps onto the window seat in the room that faces the street. She's stares with focused attention, like a mother eagle with her eye on her eaglet, as I pull my car into the driveway.

I will usually stop the car, open the window, and wave to her from below. As soon as she focuses her attention on me, she immediately darts back down the steps in anticipation of my arrival. When I open the door, there she is grinning from ear to ear (well, maybe not grinning, but undeniably very happy to see me).

On one particular day, Joe and I were in our front yard putting down mulch and cleaning up the flowerbeds. Cassy was outside with us and safely tethered to the front porch banister. She was so excited about being outside with her two-favorite people that she kept getting her leash wrapped around the shrubs and the newly planted tree. I untangled her time and time again. After the third time, I decided to put her in the house. As Joe and I continued to work, Cassy went from window to window watching our every move. I heard her whimpering every now and then as if to say, "Please let me come outside with you." She just couldn't and wouldn't settle down knowing we were so close, yet so far. Her eyes were fixed on us.

Hebrews 12:2 reminds us to do the same, "...fixing our eyes on Jesus, the Author and Perfecter of faith." By watching us, her masters, Cassy feels secure and safe because she trusts us. We take care of her; we meet her needs and we protect her and love her.

God wants us to trust Him. He promises to take care of us, meet our needs and protect and love us. In Psalm 141:8, we read, "...but my eyes are fixed on you, Sovereign Lord; in you I take refuge." Cassy obviously wants to take refuge in me and Joe, and I delight in this. However, greater is my joy knowing that I can take refuge in my Master and Creator.

Wouldn't it be wonderful if we persistently, deliberately, and exuberantly searched for God the way our dogs search for us? Shouldn't we eagerly peer through the pages of Scripture the way Cassy peers through the windows in our house? Her hope is to get a glimpse of her master as she goes from room to room leaving her smudge prints behind.

When we search for God, our Master, we too will get a glimpse of His love for us. He promises to leave His prints on our heart. Proverbs 3:1-3 says, "My son, do not forget my teaching, but keep my commands in your heart, for they will prolong your life many years and bring you peace and prosperity. Let love and faithfulness never leave you; bind them around your neck, write them on the tablet of your heart."

Can you imagine having God's love and faithfulness, His word and His Character written on your heart? He loves us more than we can imagine. I will never look at those smudges on my windows the same way again.

Chapter 8

Freedom Reigns

There is such an enormous selection of pet paraphernalia these days. Pet owners also have options for where and how to shop. There are the big-box stores, pet boutiques, or the internet where one can peruse websites specific to dogs or cats. I personally am not into clothes shopping for Cassy, but do enjoy purchasing a special treat every now and then.

Now, my girl is certainly not deprived. She has a collection of stuffed toys, rubber bouncy balls and chew sticks. Her personal favorite is her blue ball that has a squeaker in it. She will erratically bite on it with the understanding that as she chomps down, the squeaking sound is produced. She happily runs around chomping and squeaking as she goes.

Recently, I purchased a harness for Cassy because she pulls quite a bit on our walks. The harness helps to hold her back and shows her who's the *boss*. I cannot and will not give Cassy a lot of freedom outside. The terrier in her wants to run after other dogs, cats, squirrels, bunnies, birds, and any other critters she fixes her eyes on. I must leash her 95 percent of the time when we are outside. We have a five-foot leash, a six-foot leash and a retractable leash for her. All of them put us in control of how far she can go. Cassy must stay within the boundaries we set for her. If she runs off she will more than likely get herself in trouble or could possibly face injury or death.

She probably doesn't understand it like a person would, but leashes for dogs are a good thing. Just like I want to lead Cassy, God wants to lead us. The difference, however, is I *must* use a leash and collar to make her follow me. On the other hand, God gives us total freedom to follow Him or not.

Before I understood freedom, religion was like my own personal leash. My *leash of religion,* which for me was nothing more than man-made rules, felt uncomfortable and restricting. It was frustrating because I never was able to do all the things I wanted to do or thought I was required to do. I tried to be good, attended church, and do everything right, hoping to please God.

Left to herself, Cassy would follow her instinct to run and hunt after the critters in our yard. She doesn't have the awareness that we have concerning what would lead her into a dangerous situation. That is one reason I believe that God has placed us in authority over our animals.

God allows us to have the unique personal freedom to love Him, the freedom to follow Him and the freedom to live for Him. He does not want us to be leashed to Him against our will. He wants us to follow Him because of our love for Him as One who has authority over us. He knows, left to ourselves, we would follow our own desires and run after the very things that could lead us into dangerous situations. Sound familiar?

John 8:36 says, "So if the Son sets you free, you will be free indeed." Jesus also stated, "The Truth will set you free" (John 8:32). Did you know that Jesus was referring to Himself with this statement? He is The Truth (John 14:6). It's Jesus, and not the rules of religion that sets us free.

We have the freedom to love God the way we were meant to love Him. We also have the freedom to worship Him as we choose. Loving God should be as natural to us as loving our spouses, children, parents, and friends. Wow! That concept is really freeing. Who wants to be forced to love anyone? When you love someone, you naturally want to please them.

Psalm 32:9 says, "Do not be like the horse or mule, which have no understanding, but must be controlled by bit and bridle, or they will not come to you."

I will continue to keep a leash on Cassy because I love her and I know freedom for her could result in danger. I will also keep myself free from the leash of man-made rules, which could put me in danger of missing all that God has for me.

God definitely has a standard, and I intend to follow it, not because I have to, but because I want to. By not following Him, I could end up in a dangerous situation. I certainly do not want to miss out on all that He has for me; His love, joy, peace, and blessings.

Chapter 9

Cheese Doodle Feet

Cassy has her own characteristic look that is unique to her. She is beige, (I like saying champagne) but truthfully, she is just beige. She has a scruffy face and a stocky little body. She is different in her own way.

It was her cute little face; however, that drew me to her. I really wouldn't change anything about her physical look at all. I love her just the way she is. Sometimes she has one ear up and one ear down. This is very distinctively Cassy. Some might say she looks a little goofy, but I love her with my whole heart.

My good friend Joan has a flat-coat retriever named Sophie. Sophie is unique and very special to Joan. As her breed implies, Sophie's coat is not scruffy like Cassy's, but flat, shiny, and black. I think both of Sophie's ears are symmetrical also, unlike Cassy. Nonetheless, they are both dogs, yet very distinctly different from one another.

One day, Joan informed me that her dog's feet smelled like cheese doodles and asked me if I had ever sniffed Cassy's paws. I wondered why Joan would think that just because her dog has this aroma, that Cassy would? She also asked the same question of another friend, Aimee, about her dog Oreo.

Joan challenged us both to go home and smell our dog's feet to see if we could detect a cheese doodle smell. Both Aimee and I did the cheese doodle sniff test and agreed that our dogs' feet did, in fact, have the aroma of cheese doodles. The three dogs are all different, but all have cheese doodle feet!

God makes each one of us diverse as well. Some of us are tall, some are short. Some have dark skin, some light. Some have curly black hair, some have straight blonde hair. People differ greatly not only in their physical appearance, but in the way they walk, talk, and think.

Each of us is uniquely made, and no two people are exactly alike. Every individual person has their own DNA which sets them apart from anyone else. The Bible says that we were formed in the womb. Psalm 139:13 says, "For you created my inmost being; you knit me together in my mother's womb."

However, even though we may look different from one another, there are certain characteristics that we as humans share, no matter who we are or where we are from. We all have a heart, lungs, a brain, kidneys, and a liver. We cannot live without these vital organs. Some may be challenged by certain physical limitations, but God gave us our vital parts which keep us alive. He knows us intimately. Luke 12:7 says, "Indeed, the very hairs of your head are all numbered." He knows us intimately because He made us. He knows our very scent.

2 Corinthians 2:15 says, "For we are to God the pleasing aroma of Christ among those who are being saved and those who are perishing."

Just as Cassy, Oreo, and Sophie have cheese doodle feet, those that belong to Him have a scent that is unlike anything we can describe here on earth. It is the Aroma of God. We represent God when we speak, with our actions, and the way we go about our lives. Have you ever thought that you also represent Him with your aroma, the scent that you carry with you?

I hope the people I come in contact with, will find my aroma as pleasing as I find Cassy's little cheese doodle feet. I would never want my aroma to become stale smelling or foul; instead, it should be as fragrant as freshly mowed summer grass.

When I remain in Him and He remains in me I can be confident that my aroma will remain pleasing and sweet to others.

Chapter 9: Cheese Doodle Feet

Chapter 10

Toxic Treats

Even if she is in another room, Cassy can smell a treat as I am taking it out of its package. Nothing will get in her way when she knows there is a treat that has her name on it. She would probably leap tall buildings, jump into shark-infested waters, or face a pack of hungry wolves all for the love of a treat. Thankfully, for her, all she has to do is look at me with her big brown eyes and scruffy face, and she wins.

She loves freeze-dried liver and baby carrots most. If we are going on a walk, or I want to practice obedience training with her, I will grab a treat and put it in my pocket. She will undoubtedly sniff my hands and pockets as if to say, "I know you have something yummy in there." I certainly want to give her a reward, but not spoil her by giving her a treat just for being cute. She must earn it.

Recently, our son Mike was telling me that one of his college roommates was baking brownies. The smell was, well you know, "brownie-licious." I am not sure if that is a dictionary word, but it speaks volumes to those of us who love brownies. I like mine with nuts, please.

When the brownies came out of the oven, Mike and two other buddies went into the kitchen to get some. They were not the only ones ready to chow down on these delicious chocolate brownies. Mojo and Zoe, although uninvited, tagged along.

They are the two black labs that belong to Mike's roommates. With their tails wagging, noses sniffing, and lips smacking, they were intent on eating whatever this glorious scent was that drew them into the kitchen. The brownies smelled good to everyone. They were hoping to get a piece or even a few crumbs that might fall to the floor. The problem is that chocolate is toxic to dogs. However, they don't know this. All they know is how great they smell. What could be so harmful about a brownie? After all, it's not like giving your dog chemicals or fertilizer to eat. It's a brownie!

The same may be true for us. Things that may seem absolutely harmless can be very *toxic* to us, to our reputation, or even to our families. In the very beginning, man was tempted by a seemingly harmless piece of fruit. God told Adam and Eve that they may not eat from the one tree He designated as the Tree of Knowledge of Good and Evil (Genesis 2:17). What did Adam and Eve do? They took the forbidden fruit from the one tree that was off limits.

I suspect that God placed the tree there so Adam could choose whether to obey Him. If he hadn't taken the fruit, I believe this would have proven his love and obedience toward God. Since he chose to take it, Adam's rebellion and disobedience were revealed. We usually want to please those we love. Perhaps God had to provide an opportunity to give Adam the choice of obedience or disobedience.

Although the parallels between the toxic chocolate for dogs and the toxic things that can pollute our lives are similar, there is one big difference. We have control over what our dogs eat. We have authority over what they can ingest. We know what is good for our pets, and would certainly not give chocolate or any other harmful thing to them purposefully.

God knows what is and is not good for us as well. His desire is for us to refrain from ingesting things that will leave a lingering toxicity in our lives. We must choose to ignore the sweet smells, fatal attractions, or constant distractions vying for our attention. As we follow God, I believe we will lose the desire for those things in life that could harm us. John 10:3-4 reminds us of this. Jesus says, "He calls His sheep [us] by name." His sheep follow Him because they know His voice. Let's listen to the Good Shepherd. He has many treats for us that are good, satisfying and fulfilling.

Yes, Cassy loves freeze-dried liver and baby carrots. Our Master has far more than liver and carrots for us. He will not only give us what we want, but He promises to give us more than we could ask for or imagine (Ephesians 3:20). I think I'll go and bake some brownies. I'll have mine with nuts, please.

Chapter 11

Did I Do That?

What is blue, bouncy, squeaky, and irresistible to Cassy? Her favorite ball is, of course. It had goofy black eyes and nubby little feet, but she chewed them off. Her blue ball is her most prized possession.

Cassy has figured out that if she goes to the top of the staircase, she can push her ball down the steps with her nose. It will erratically bounce and squeak down each step before landing on the floor below. She created this game so that she can play all by herself.

This game will entertain her sometimes for up to 15 or 20 minutes. Cassy also purposely pushes her ball under the couch in the living room or the armoire in my bedroom. She will then frantically attempt to retrieve it with her paws or mouth. Her attempts are mostly unsuccessful. She will moan, cry or bark while staring under the furniture as if to say, "Help, my ball is stuck, and I can't get it." Joe or I will crawl onto the floor, feel under the furniture until we grasp the ball, and then we give it back to her. This will continue on and on until this game is no longer any fun for me or Joe. We will sternly look at her and say in a loud voice, "NO," but because she's a puppy, she continues to push her ball under the furniture on purpose. Cassy will do this even though she knows she shouldn't.

It was the apostle Paul who said in Romans 7:17-18, "As it is, it is no longer I myself who do it, but it is sin living in me. For I know that good itself does not dwell in me, that is, in my sinful nature. For I have the desire to do what is good, but I cannot carry it out."

I believe that Cassy's behavior of purposefully pushing her ball into tight spaces is not a sinful act. She is not capable of knowing the difference. She instinctively tries to dig for her ball that is wedged deeply under the furniture because it is fun and she is a terrier. Terriers are known for this digging behavior.

I usually just take her ball and put it out of her reach. My hope is that she will get the message and stop doing what I don't want her to do. Inevitably, I give her the ball back, and there she goes again; doing what she knows she shouldn't do.

I like to read about the apostle Paul because I can relate to the very struggles that he faced. I am glad he revealed his true nature repeatedly throughout the book of Romans. After all, he is the famous Paul of the Bible, and even he fell short. I think it was Paul's transparency that allowed him to be used so greatly by The Lord.

He knew the secret to living victoriously for God's Kingdom, and he shares that secret with us in Romans 6:12, 14. "Therefore, do not let sin reign in your mortal body so that you obey its evil desires. For sin shall no longer be your master." Now that Cassy is a bit older and past the puppy stage, she no longer purposely pushes her ball into tight spots because she knows this behavior doesn't cultivate a positive reaction from her masters. She doesn't like hearing the words, "no" or "stop that" or even worse, "that's enough; no more ball."

I believe the same holds true for us. When we continually do what we know goes against God's standard, positive results are never cultivated in us or by us. Like the apostle Paul we wind up doing the very things we don't want to do and not doing the things we know we should. I love that, when we turn from our sin and turn to God, the results are always good. 1John 1:9 says, "If we confess our sins, He is faithful and just and will forgive us our sins and purify us from all unrighteousness."

When Cassy misbehaves, she gets a correction by us. Like a sheepish looking child who denies taking a cookie from the cookie jar (even though there are crumbs in the bed), her eyes look sad and her ears go way down when she knows she did wrong. She would much rather hear, "good girl" and know a belly rub is on its way.

Just like Cassy, I do not want to disappoint my Master.

Even though I fail at times, I know that God's forgiveness is in ample supply. Someday I want to hear the words, "Well done, good and faithful servant!" (Matthew 25:23). Like Cassy, I also hope to hear, "good girl."

But please, no belly rubs for me.

Chapter 12

In the Warmth of The Son

Cassy spends a little time every day eating, playing, snuggling, and sleeping. Some days, like most dogs, she sleeps more than she does anything else. Most of her days are spent with my husband Joe since he works from home. Joe spends a good amount of time in front of his computer, which is upstairs, or in his studio, which is downstairs. Depending on what he is working on, he may have to move from one floor to the other, which means he doesn't always know Cassy's whereabouts in the house. Because she still has pup in her, we've discovered it is a good idea to check on her every so often to make sure she hasn't entered into "The Danger Zone."

Most days Joe doesn't have to look very far for her, especially if it's a bright sunny day. He knows he will find her basking in the warm radiance of the sun coming through the front window of our house.

As the hours progress through the day, and the sun changes direction, Cassy will find just the right sunny spot. She can be found curled up on one of the steps on the front hall staircase depending on which one the sun is shining. She will often move up the steps as she follows the sun. I am not sure if it is the warmth or the brightness of the sun that attracts her. Perhaps it is both.

Jesus refers to himself as "The Light of the World" (John 8:12). Light and dark cannot exist together. Even a very small lantern, a lighted match or one lit candle in a dark room expels the darkness; so it is with The Lord. In Psalm 119:105 we read, "Your Word is a lamp for my feet and a light on my path." The Bible tells us that Jesus is The Light, and He is also The Word.

John 1:1, "In the beginning was The Word, and The Word was with God and The Word was God." This tells me that The Word, Jesus, came to be Light for us. Just as the sun lights up the world physically, Jesus, The Son, came to light up the world spiritually.

If God had not created the solar system and placed the sun in the sky to give us light and warmth, this world would be dark, cold, and lifeless, but thanks be to God, He did. Without the sun, our land, water, and air would freeze. Survival of mankind, plants, or animal life as we know it, would be impossible.

Spending ten years in New England was a lot colder than I could tolerate, but the absence of the sun would make New England in January seem more like Antarctica. How wonderful it is to wake up each day and not have to worry whether or not the sun is still up in the sky. Our Father has us covered.

The Bible tells us that before salvation, our hearts are darkened, and we are spiritually dead. For the Christian believer, The Light is what gives us life. Colossians 1:13 says, "For He has rescued us from the dominion of darkness and brought us into the kingdom of the Son He loves."

Cassy loves nothing more than to bask in the warmth and light from the sun. To her, lying on the sun-soaked steps of our staircase is like being a celebrity lying on the famously glamorous hot sands of the French Riviera. Her soft, pretty, champagne-colored coat shines brilliantly from the glow of the sunlight on her little body. She looks pleasantly content as she lies in the radiant heat from the sun.

Cassy is one smart pup to choose the light and warmth that the sun delivers to the staircase each day. She knows her daily spot provides security, rest, and comfort. Like Cassy, I also desire security, rest, and comfort. For me, it is found in the brightest of all light, The Son, The Life Giver, The Light of The World—Jesus Christ!

Chapter 13

Perfectly Happy

Have you ever been around a dog that was living with a deformity or illness? If you have, you may have noticed that they don't complain much and typically accept it cheerfully. Thankfully, Cassy is healthy, vibrant, and full of energy. She has full use of her four paws and can run like the dickens.

One time I recall accidentally stepping on one of Cassy's paws and hearing a small miserable squeak, but she quickly recovered both physically and emotionally. She was not angry with me even though it was my fault for not looking where I was going. As I scooped down to comfort her, she began licking me and wagging her tail with not even a hint of resentment. This is not always the case with people.

Recently, my friend Prema told me that her family's dog, Penny, was accidentally injured by a family member who stepped on her little eight-pound body. It resulted in a broken hip and leg. Little Penny had to have surgery that helped, but was not successful in freeing her of her lameness. Penny, now six months old, lives with a deformed leg and hip. She is handicapped and limited in her mobility. Penny is not angry; she plays like any other pup, and she desires to please her master. She lives life perfectly happy, in spite of her weakness. She doesn't appear to blame anyone and never complains that she is not like the other pups of the world. She doesn't demand special attention and has never once asked to be pitied. It is not clear if Penny even knows that she is different.

While visiting her family six months after Penny's accident, Prema called to give me an update on Penny's recovery. "Penny is so happy. Her spirit is amazing even though she has obvious deformities." Apparently, Penny has learned how to run and play without putting her full body weight on her deformed leg. Her disability certainly has not compromised her ability to live out her life like any other little miniature pincher.

2 Corinthians 12:9 says, "My grace is sufficient for you, for my power is made perfect in weakness. Therefore, I will boast all the more gladly about my weaknesses, so that Christ's power may rest on me." The apostle Paul apparently understood what it meant to rise above his circumstances. It is almost like Penny understood what Paul was saying. It is obvious that she is not cognitively aware of what the Scriptures tell us, but her instinctive behavior to rise above her difficulty is apparent to everyone who knows her. I wonder, is it possible that God has chosen to use animals to show us what He meant in the following verse? "Consider it pure joy, my brothers and sisters, whenever you face trials of many kinds" (James 1:2).

Have you ever wondered what the world would be like if no one complained about physical or emotional difficulties, financial problems, family problems or any other challenges that we all face from time to time? I think it would be glorious. I believe that complaining will not exist in Heaven. The Bible says there will be no more tears, no more pain, no more death or mourning in Heaven (Revelation 21:4). Penny appears to be living her life as if she were already in Heaven.

Do you think it is possible to live life joyfully in spite of our difficulties? Penny does. Jesus reminds us in Matthew 5:8, "Blessed [oh how happy] are the pure in heart, for they shall see God." Just as a little yeast works through the whole batch of dough, perhaps a little joy might work through a whole lot of bitterness. Penny's great disposition in spite of her disability reflects Gods desire for us. Next time I am tempted to grumble about something that is not what I expected or wanted for my life, I will try thinking about Penny, the *mighty min pin*.

Chapter 13: Perfectly Happy

Chapter 14

The Destroyer

Cassy rarely chewed on or destroyed anything in our home as a young pup. I did share previously about how she was unknowingly rewarded for chewing a pillow sham on my bed. Thankfully, that was an isolated incident she has yet to repeat. She has been a really good girl.

Although she may not have destroyed our things, her things are a different story. Give her a stuffed toy, especially the kind with a squeaker in it and it is sure to only have about a twenty-minute life expectancy. She will take the toy in her mouth and tear, rip, mutilate, decapitate, and amputate it all within minutes. Her ultimate goal is to get to the squeaker. Like a skilled cardiac thoracic surgeon, she goes right to the heart of the matter. She will pull all the stuffing out, and let me tell you, there is a *lot* of stuffing in a stuffed toy.

Joe and I decided to purchase only inexpensive stuffed toys for her since we know all about her destroyer capabilities. We basically buy them knowing they will be destroyed before throwing them away. Every stuffed toy that Cassy gets her paws on is certain to meet an early demise. She doesn't show any sign of attachment to these stuffed toys. She does; however, show great attachment to her bed, her blue ball, and her family. These she will never bite or chew on. She knows what is important and whom she loves.

Matthew 6:19-20 tells us, "Do not store up for yourselves treasures on earth, where moths and vermin destroy, and where thieves break in and steal. But store up for yourselves treasures in heaven, where moth and vermin do not destroy, and where thieves do not break in and steal."

Jesus' life on earth was an example for us to learn how to store up treasures in Heaven. There is no mention in the Scriptures of Jesus' things. Perhaps He didn't have a lot of personal items, or if He did, I don't think He was attached to them. The Bible says He didn't have a home, a bed to lay His head on or any other earthly treasures. He could have had anything He wanted; after all, He is God. He had everything He needed, and it wasn't things. What He did have was important to Him, which was the love of His mother, brothers, disciples, and His followers. Most of all, He had the love and approval of His Father in Heaven, who was "well pleased with Him" (Matthew 3:17).

Cassy's stuffed toys are not her life's treasures, and that is why I believe she destroys them. Her life's treasures are me, Joe, and our children. We are everything to her. To Cassy, we are rock stars, celebrities, kings, queens and maybe even bigger than life itself. She loves us with a capital "L." Her love is unconditional and unwavering.

"Where our treasure is, there our heart will also be" (Luke 12:34). Where is your heart? What is your treasure? I do not want to store up earthly treasures that have no eternal value like Cassy's stuffed toys. I want to store up heavenly treasures that will never be destroyed, ruined or decay and whose values are everlasting and of great worth. The relationships I have with my family, friends and The Lord are my heart's treasures and their eternal value, worth more than silver or gold, make me one very wealthy lady.

Chapter 14: The Destroyer

Chapter 15

It is Better to Give than to Receive

I didn't become a dog mom until I was in my mid-forties. Sad, I know! However, now that I am a dog mom, I can honestly say that I have become the very person I once made fun of. You know the type—crazy dog people. Call it ignorance, pride, or whatever you want. I just didn't know. I was clueless and totally uninformed about the joys of pet ownership.

Before I got Cassy, I thought about all the things I would want to give her. I would certainly give her food, water, discipline, love, toys, treats, and a comfortable home. After all, I was the human and could provide all that she needed. I imagined that she could provide me with companionship (when I needed it) and the warm, cozy, fuzzy feelings I can remember experiencing as a young child when I cuddled with my stuffed monkey, Fungi.

As you might expect, many of my well-meaning friends and family members advised me to think long and hard about the decision to bring a dog into my life. They were quick to remind me that my kids were growing up and preparing to leave the nest. What would it be like to suddenly be tied down to a dog? What would we do with her if we wanted to travel? If we were out for several hours or more, I would have to plan for someone to come into our home and give our dog food, water and potty breaks. Hmmm, I really had to give this a lot of thought. Maybe dog ownership is more than I really wanted to sign up for.

After much deliberation and family discussion, I decided that since our travel time is so minimal, (about two weeks per year) then this wasn't a justifiable reason to not bring a dog into our life. After all, I could give a dog everything he/she needed and so much more, right?

After years of owning Cassy, I can proudly say that I have followed through on my initial plan to give her all she needs and wants. Her life is so simple. All she requires besides her basic need for food, water, and potty breaks, are her mom, dad, brothers, sister, blue ball, and an occasional cookie. That's it! Heck, we can give her these. She receives lots of love, belly rubs and exercise when my son Jarett throws her ball in the yard. She loves to chase and retrieve it. Life for Cassy is good. If she could talk, she might say, "La dolce vita," the sweet life.

What occurred over the past several years can only be described as a phenomenon that almost all pet owners can understand. I realized that although I give Cassy so much, she gives far more than she receives. Obviously, she is not capable of giving me material things, but she continually, graciously, and loyally gives companionship, attention, protection, and faithful love. Her eyes are always on her master, and her heart is constantly centered on pleasing me. I was caught up in what I could do for her while she was focused on blessing me, and what a blessing it has been.

Jesus graciously taught His disciples this principle, "It is more blessed to give than to receive" (Acts 20:35). And once again, I see tremendous similarities to the awesome relationship my Master desires from me and the relationship Cassy demonstrates to me. God's word says that, "…the greatest of all the commandments is to Love the Lord your God with all your heart, with all your soul and with all your mind" (Mark 12:30).

Think about that. When we follow this commandment, everything else will fall into its proper place in our lives. How can it not? How can we love God with our entire heart, soul and mind and be mean-spirited and unkind at the same time? Cassy loves me with her entire being, right down to her waggly tail. She doesn't know what it is to be mean and unkind. These qualities are foreign to her.

Perhaps loving God first and foremost will help to diminish our sometimes-unlovely character traits. It brings Him great joy when we give our heart, soul, and mind to Him. I believe that in giving ourselves to Him, we receive more than we can ask, more than we need and more than we can imagine. We receive Him! When I ponder His gift of grace toward me, I too can say, "La dolce vita, life IS sweet."

Chapter 15: It is Better to Give than to Receive

Chapter 16

Zero to Sixty

When Cassy was a little over two years old, she spent a good amount of time sleeping. She still has a lot of pup in her, but this dog can sleep. She gives credibility to the phrase, "slept like a log."

Her mornings are particularly quiet. She will eat, do her business, and then cozy up in her bed or on mine. On any typical morning, she can also be found in the warm sunny spot on the front staircase steps.

She awakens in the late afternoon, usually because family members are coming home, and she gets lots of attention. I am always amazed at how sharp her sense of hearing is. She can be sound asleep in one room and still hear the subtle squeak of her favorite blue ball that was accidentally moved by someone entering another room. She will literally go from sleeping to completely awake, jump to her feet, and run on all fours to the location of the squeak—zero to sixty.

Now, when I wake up, it is usually a process, a slow process. I wish I could be as nimble as Cassy. She runs to whomever and whatever excites her. Her acute hearing skills prompt her to respond without hesitation. She is always listening, even when she appears to be asleep. She has a very quick reaction time. She runs so fast that you can almost see smoke trailing from her hind paws.

The Lord wants us to have a very quick reaction time also. He tells us to "be quick to listen and slow to speak" (James 1:19). So often I mix this up. I am quick to speak and slow to listen. Just ask my husband Joe, or our children. They will wholeheartedly attest that!

1 Corinthians 9:24 says, "Do you not know that in a race all the runners run, but only one gets the prize?" Run in such a way as to get the prize. We get to choose whether we will walk, run or not move at all. Cassy doesn't have to be coaxed to run. She just goes with her impulse; she instinctively reacts. When God calls us to do something, to say something or respond obediently in some way, do we react? Do we run to the very sound of His voice? Proverbs 18:10 says, "The name of the Lord is a fortified tower; the righteous run to it and they are safe."

Cassy runs to us at the very sound of Joe's or my voice. There is no hesitation. We call, and she comes to her masters—zero to sixty.

I think we should respond in the same way to the One who calls us. Let's be slow to speak, quick to listen and eager to run the race He calls us to be part of.

Chapter 17

Tell Tale Signs

Have you ever thought about how many different breeds of dogs there are? Dogs truly come in all shapes, sizes, and colors. There is the tiny Chihuahua, the gigantic Great Dane, the muscular Boxer, the short and stout Dachshund, the French Poodle, and the strong Pit Bull. There are teacup size, miniatures, large breeds, and giant breeds. They are all different, but all are members of the canine family.

Just as they have differing body styles and sizes, they also have different tails. Stubby, long, short, furry, docked, straight and curled, just to name a few. Although physically different, all dogs use their tails to communicate with other dogs and with humans. When a dog has its tail between his legs, this generally is a sign of fear or timidity. A stiff straight tail might mean aggression. All of us have seen the delightful wagging tail and know that this is a clear sign of excitement or happiness. My dog Cassy has a short stocky tail that she wags very quickly back and forth. She tells me how happy she is almost all the time. She can't hide her excitement. It's written all over her tail!

I heard a story about a group of poker players who gathered around a large game table. The room they were in was quiet, except for the sound of the cards being shuffled and dealt. One of the players was a medium-sized, mixed-breed mutt. He was the only dog in this group of cigar-smoking guys. The furry four-legged player had just been dealt a very good hand which made him quite happy. One of the guys looked at him and said, "Your problem is not your poker face, it's your poker tail!" He obviously couldn't contain his excitement and it showed. His wagging tail was a sure sign of his winning hand.

As children of God, we are told to let our light shine before men. We are encouraged to allow others to see in us the joy that comes from being at peace with God. The world is looking at us and how we respond to the hand we have been dealt in life. What do others see when looking to you and me?

There are always going to be seasons of plenty and seasons of want. When we are on the mountaintop and things are going well, it is easy to let our light shine brightly. But how about the times when we are in the valley? It's hard to be a light when we are not full of joy.

Like me, you may wonder, "How can I let my light shine when I feel as though I'm alone, confused or just not where I want to be." I think we should look to the apostle Paul. He said that he learned to be content whatever the circumstances. He knew what it is to be in need, and he knew what it was to have plenty. He learned the secret of being content in any and every situation, whether well fed or hungry, whether living in plenty or in want (Philippians 4:11-12).

In Acts 16:24-25, we are told that Paul and Silas were jailed in a dungeon with their feet in stocks. Paul and Silas were praying and singing hymns to God and the other prisoners were listening to them. Paul and Silas couldn't contain their joy. They let their light shine in spite of their circumstances.

When Cassy is in the presence of her masters, she cannot contain her joy either. Her short stubby tail gives it away. My hope is that the joy of the Lord will be the telltale sign of my life. I want others to see the brilliance of His light reflected daily through me in all I say and all I do in spite of my circumstances. Like Cassy, I need to sit and stay in the presence of my Master.

Chapter 17: Tell Tale Signs

Chapter 18

O.L.D. (Obsessive Licking Disorder)

If I had a penny for every kiss Cassy has given me in the two and a half years since I've owned her, I would be a very wealthy lady. I don't know if I would make it into the *Forbes Magazine* list of richest females, but I certainly believe I would be neck and neck with those that are. Besides her constant wagging tail, she is very generous with her love and kisses. She will lick me until I can no longer take it and tell her, "no more." There are times when she will be lying down with her eyes closed, and she will lick the couch, bed, or whatever surface she is lying on. Like a child who finds comfort in thumb sucking, Cassy seems to find comfort in licking.

While lying next to our son Jarett one evening, Cassy began to lick his hand over and over. It was Jarett who jokingly said, "Cassy has obsessive licking disorder, O.L.D." Her licking persists until she finally relaxes and drifts off to sleep. Simply put, she finds comfort in her master.

The Lord is delighted when His children find comfort in Him also. He is always available and always accessible. It was not uncommon for the disciples to recline with The Lord and find comfort in His mere presence. In 1 Peter 5:7 we read, "Cast your anxiety on Him because He cares for you" and in Psalm 119:76 it says, "May your unfailing love be my comfort."

Before Jesus left earth to return to His heavenly home, He promised to send the Holy Spirit. The Holy Spirit is our counselor and our comforter. Jesus assures all believers that we will not be left as orphans (John 14:18). "As a mother comforts her child, so I will comfort you" (Isaiah 66:13).

Like Cassy, I believe we all need comfort. We need to find a way of letting go of those things that try to rob us of our peace. Listening to praise music is a great way for me to "let go and let God." At other times, I find reading and meditating on the psalms or praying is just what I need to go from woeful to joyful.

Cassy licks as a way to relax and be comforted. This behavior typically precedes undisturbed, peaceful sleep. Jesus wants to be our comforter. "He is The Prince of Peace" (Isaiah 9:6). It is in Proverbs 3:24 that we read, "When you lie down, you will not be afraid; when you lie down your sleep will be sweet." How comforting is this? We are all invited to relax in His presence, so join me as we sit with our Master and enjoy the comfort He provides. But please, no licking allowed.

Chapter 19

Scoopy Lulu

Do you have crazy pet names for your dog? We call Cassy by her name, but we also call her other names like Scoopy, Lulu, and Scoopy Doopy. It is just another expression of our love for her. The funny thing is, she responds to all of these names. When Cassy misbehaves, (like the time she chewed my pillow sham) I do not call her Scoopy or Lulu. My tone and voice volume as I shout "Cassy," lets her know I'm not in the Scoopy Doopy mood. She will reluctantly approach me with her ears pinned back, tail down and a deliberately slow-paced walk. She knows she is in big trouble. It takes every bit of me not to swoop her up into my arms and tell her "It's OK; I still love you." No! I have to be firm, even though her droopy ears and eyes are melting me. I usually make her go to her bed. Her sluggish walk and body language alone tell me she knows she did something wrong.

How different it is when she is ready to play, or when we enter the house and she eagerly runs to greet us. With her tail wagging at lightning speed, she will enthusiastically bring us her ball that is held tightly between her teeth. Sometimes she will have one ear up and the other down. You see her body language also communicates happiness and excitement. That's when all the silly talk happens, and we start calling her names other than Cassy.

I have different names for Cassy depending on my mood. When I am excited and happy to see her, I usually call her Scoopy. "Come on Scoopy" or "Let's go Lulu, get your ball." When I am tired or just not in a playful mood, I am more inclined to say, "Come on Cas" or "Cassy, come here." I would never call someone else's dog a silly pet name after just meeting him or her. It's sort of a personal thing between a pet and their master.

I have noticed that the same is true when referring to or addressing God. Many people refer to Him as God or Father or maybe even Lord. These are all wonderful expressions of our Creator. Did you know that God has many other names that are revealed in the Scriptures? He invites us to use these names as we pray, worship or refer to Him when speaking to others. There are many more names for God than I can list in this passage, but some of my favorite names are;

1. The Way. John 14:6 "I am the Way, The Truth and The Life."
2. The Light of The World. John 8:12 (darkness disappears in the light)
3. The Bread of Life. John 6:35 (He will satisfy your hungry heart)
4. The Living Water. John 7:38 (He will quench your thirsty soul)

5. The Alpha and The Omega. Rev. 22:13 (The Beginning and The End)
6. The Lamb of God. John 1:29 (He became our perfect Sacrifice)
7. The Vine. John 15:5 (If we stay connected to The Vine, we will bear much fruit)
8. Abba. Romans 8:15 (a more intimate name, similar to "Daddy")
9. Jehovah-Jireh. Genesis 22:14 (my favorite of all, "The Lord will Provide")

Once again, my mood generally determines what name I might use when calling upon God. You see, when I am frustrated, unhappy, or upset, I am more likely to respond by saying, "Why God? How can this be Father?" When I am happy and remain connected to The Vine, my responses are more intimate and personal, such as, "Thank you Father for being my Bread of Life and Living Water. Thank you also for being my Abba Father and Jehovah-Jireh." What a joy it is to know that as a child of The King of Kings and Creator of Heaven and Earth, I can be comfortable approaching Him, my Master, with these wonderful expressions of love for Him.

Whatever names we use to call upon God, I believe it is not our words, but our hearts that truly matter. He loves us and calls us His children. He says we are blessed and precious in His sight. In Jeremiah 33:3, He invites us to call Him. "Call to me and I will answer you and tell you great and unsearchable things you do not know." Why not give Him a call today!

Chapter 20

To Need or Not to Need

We feed Cassy twice daily, morning and evening. She continually has fresh clean water in her bowl and always responds to her need to go potty. Cassy gets lots of belly rubs from everyone in our family, and she is told numerous times a day how cute she is. We are very diligent about keeping her exercised and fit. We love our pet and want her to live a long healthy life. We try to give her everything she needs.

We also give Cassy lots of things she doesn't need. Perhaps this sounds a bit confusing since all of her basic needs for food, water, exercise and physical safety are being met. If we provide all the above, then why would we also give our precious pup things she has no need for? After all, what else is there that she doesn't already have?

We like to buy Cassy toys from our local pet discount store. She has a variety of plush toys (for destroying), balls for chasing and sticks for chewing. The funny thing is, she seems perfectly content with the toys she already has and doesn't ask for anything new. I will often take her to the pet discount store with me and together we will walk up and down the aisles which are filled with toys, clothes, and supplies specifically designed for dogs. I peruse these aisles in an attempt to find what I think Cassy will want. I squeeze, feel, poke, pull and even smell some of the toys in an attempt to find the perfect one. I also show them to Cassy hoping that she will shed some light on my decision making.

Am I nuts? Have I lost my mind or am I just a victim of marketing madness from the pet store giants? Whatever the case may be, it is not Cassy who wants something new; it is me who wants her to have something new. I must learn to better distinguish between wants and needs. I probably should pull out and study the "Basic Needs 101" manual for dog owners and stay out of the pet discount store.

Does Cassy really need to have a toy box full of toys? Does she need doggie treats in a variety of favors such as chicken, liver, beef, duck, salmon, or breath-freshening mint? The answer is no, but I give her these things because I get enjoyment out of treating our dog and rewarding her for the loyal companionship she gives us. I not only supply her needs, but I give her things she doesn't need.

God supplies all that we need as well. We are able to live and move and have our being, (Acts 17:28) all by His grace. However, it doesn't stop there. Because of His great love for His children, He also allows us to have so much more than we need. Philippians 4:19 says, "And my God will meet all your needs according to His glorious riches in Christ Jesus." Do we really need big-screen TV's and multiple cars in our driveways? Probably not, but He blesses us with these things anyway. I know I can certainly live without many of my earthly treasures, but I get to enjoy lots of things that I have no need of. Philippians 4:12 says, "I know what it is to be in need and I know what it is to have plenty. I have learned the secret of being content in any and every situation whether well fed or hungry, whether living in plenty or in want."

The greatest gift God gave to us was His Son, Jesus. God knew we would need salvation and He provided a way for us to be reconciled to Himself through the cross. He knew we would need direction and guidance; therefore, He graciously gave us His written word, the Bible, to help us navigate through life.

All we need and all we have is from God. Cassy is a gift from Him to our family. We didn't need a dog; we wanted a dog, and God has blessed us with her.

Matthew 7:11 says, "If you then, though you are evil, know how to give good gifts to your children, how much more will your Father in Heaven give good gifts to those who ask Him!"

Chapter 20: To Need or Not to Need

Chapter 21

Gentle Leader

Cassy has a variety of collars and leashes. Most of the time we put a harness on her before we go on a walk, but we have also tried a Gentle Leader, which is a type of leash that goes around her muzzle instead of her neck or shoulders. When she pulls forward, a gentle tug of the lead gives a little correction and usually will get her attention without causing injury to her neck. I like the concept of gentle correction to refocus her attention. I call this *calm assertive discipline* .

Most experts would agree that this approach is far better than yelling, scolding, hitting, or showing angry aggression to gain your dog's obedience, which does nothing but intensify negative behavior. Proper discipline will not only produce obedience, but will insure your dog's safety, keep them happy, and in turn, make their owners happy as well.

Jesus is our Gentle Leader. His discipline toward us is out of a heart of love. In Hebrews 12:5-6, we read, "My son, do not make light of the Lord's discipline, and do not lose heart when He rebukes you, because the Lord disciplines the one He loves and chastens everyone He accepts as His son."

In the story of the prodigal son, the young man chose to disobey his father and went away with wrong motives and desires. He squandered his inheritance. He shamed his family name, made poor choices and ruined his reputation.

After realizing his folly, and knowing that even his father's hired servants were treated better than he was, he decided to return to his father and beg for forgiveness.

Perhaps the Lord was tugging on his heart, or perhaps it was his intense need for physical nourishment that brought him to his senses. After all, he came to the realization that his father's servants were eating healthier than him. "How many of my father's hired servants have food to spare, and here I am starving to death" (Luke 15:17)? He knew he had rebelled against his father and Heaven and expressed his unworthiness. "I will set out and go back to my father and say to him: Father, I have sinned against heaven and against you" (Luke 15:18-19).

We read in this story how the father welcomed his son back home, threw a party in his son's honor and showered him with love. Why? His son was going in the wrong direction and chose to come back. Whether this return to the father was driven by starvation or the tugging on his heart by God, we only know that he returned.

The father in this story didn't humiliate or degrade his son. In fact, there is no mention of the father's anger. Instead, he joyfully received his son back and reconciled him into the family.

Ephesians 6:4 says, "Fathers, do not exasperate your children; instead, bring them up in the training and instruction of the Lord."

All of us who belong to Jesus were going in the wrong direction before salvation. When our eyes were opened to our need for a savior because of our sin, and we believed in and accepted Jesus as the Son of God, then He welcomed us home and joyfully forgave us. Every one of us can be compared to the prodigal son if we have accepted Jesus as our Savior. When we are living in disobedience towards God, He gently leads us to Himself.

God never humiliates us, degrades us or turns His back on us. Thankfully, most of us never get what we deserve. If we did, we would still be going in the wrong direction. He is our Gentle Leader. A little correction may be all some of us need. Still others may need years and years of gentle correction before they willingly obey His call.

When we respond to His invitation to come into the family of God through the sacrifice Jesus made on our behalf, He opens His arms to receive us. He gives us gifts to celebrate: salvation, eternity, and a dwelling place in heaven. We gain the fruits of the Spirit: love, joy, peace, patience, kindness, goodness, faithfulness, gentleness, and self-control (Galatians 5:22). Now this is worth celebrating! I am glad that I am a prodigal child who responded to my Gentle Leader. I hope you have or will.

Chapter 21: Gentle Leader

Chapter 22

Thirst No More

Soon after we got Cassy, we visited the veterinarian for a complete puppy checkup. Just like going to the pediatrician for the first time with our babies, we were now getting dog parenting instructions. We listened intently as Dr. Jennifer reviewed with us the "dos and don'ts" of puppyhood. One thing she stressed was the importance of always having a bowl of water for our dog to drink. Ever since her early days, Cassy is sure to find her bowl filled with fresh clean water. Some days, especially in the summer months, she will lap up the entire contents of the water in her bowl. She doesn't *tell* us her bowl is empty; Joe and I will just notice it is dry and we will fill it back up.

One very hot Saturday in June, we were visiting friends for a backyard cookout. Mojo and Zoe were there. They are two of Cassy's friends. Both are black labs born from the same litter. They didn't exactly receive an invitation to the cookout, but since it was their owner's home, they were of course, in attendance.

There must have been thirty people at this gathering, and it seemed most of them thought Mojo and Zoe were there to receive love and attention. So naturally, the two dogs were having a great time. One thing about labs is their insatiable desire for play. All this playing on a hot June day will make any dog thirsty.

Soon the dogs began to heat up and their activity slowed. Their tails were drooping and tongues hanging out. As if on cue, they followed one another into the house for a refreshing drink of cool water. Slurp, slurp, lap, lap. The water splashed as the two black Labradors gulped down every bit of water with their big pink tongues, only stopping to breathe.

Panting heavily, with slobber on their faces, they both picked up their empty bowls with their mouths. I wondered what they were doing! They trotted outside and went right to their master who was at the grill. They both stood there, almost breathless from all their slurping, with their bowls hanging out of their mouths begging for more water. They knew just where to go for a refill. Their thirst had not been fully quenched; therefore, they needed more water.

Jesus told the Samaritan woman, whom He had met at the well, that the water He had was living water (John 4: 10), and all who drink it would never thirst again (John 4:13-14).

Before Jesus spoke of the living water, He said all who drink of the water from the well will continue to thirst. Naturally, our need for water, as well as our dogs' need for water, must be met. Cassy, Mojo, and Zoe will have to keep going back for more water as this physical requirement never ends.

Water is something everyone needs and everybody can relate to. Retrieving water from a well was something this Samaritan woman did daily for her family, herself, and her animals. The physical requirement for water had to be met each day and on this particular day, she encountered Jesus as He was traveling through Samaria.

We learn from this passage that Jesus was tired and thirsty. He asked her for a drink of water (John 4:7). Although this woman was there to retrieve water that day, Jesus, through His conversation with her, saw her greater spiritual need and spoke to her about a *different kind of water* . John 4:13-14 says, "Everyone who drinks this water will be thirsty again, but whoever drinks the water I give them will never thirst. Indeed, the water I give them will become in them a spring of water welling up to eternal life." Jesus used the simple things of life to teach us profound truths.

Mojo and Zoe's thirst has to be continually *quenched,* and they know who their source for water is. They go to their master. We need our spiritual thirst to be continually quenched. We know how to meet our physical need for water; we turn on the faucet, open a bottle or stand outside with our mouth opened wide during a rainstorm. I prefer to keep a chilled carafe of water in the refrigerator.

Jesus tells us how to fulfill our spiritual need. He tells us to come to Him for water that will quench our spiritual thirst and keep us continually refreshed.

Let's go to our Master when we are thirsty. He promises living water which is sure to satisfy. He welcomes all who come to Him and all who are in need of spiritual refreshment. Mojo and Zoe were breathless as they begged their master for water. I hope my desire for Living Water would leave me breathlessly in need until it is met by Jesus, the only One who satisfies.

Psalm 42:1 says, "As the deer pants for streams of water, so my soul pants for you, my God."

Chapter 23

Don't Fence Me In

Cassy is not only cute; she also has skills. She can chase a furry critter and then disappear into the next yard so fast she makes my head spin like a merry-go-round. My heart leaps from my chest, when I see her backside exiting our yard at top speed with her eyes focused on her prey. Her vanishing acts get me a little frantic when I cannot see where she has disappeared. As I gain control over my frenzied state, I begin a search and rescue attempt to bring her home.

Cassy has no fear and forgets all boundaries I have set for her when there is a critter involved. Although she is having fun, I worry about her safety. We have a large storm drain in the back of our property (that snakes and other not so lovely living things, occupy), and I cringe over the thought of her going into it. I am not the most adventurous type, but Cassy is. I want her to have fun outside, but I also want her to be safe. I knew that putting up a fence would thwart her escape tactics and give me a sense of peace.

I asked Joe if we could fence in a part of the yard. After some (persistent) coaxing, I finally got the fence. Now Cassy can go out the back door and roll in the grass, chase birds and bunnies, lie in the sun and run to her heart's delight without gaining access to the woods, the street, or the terrifyingly creepy storm drain. I can relax knowing she is safe.

As her master, it is my duty to protect her. I want to provide a safe environment for her. She needed a fence to mark out the boundaries to show her the limits I set for her. I cannot reason with her or give her a verbal warning as to how far she can go. I had to provide an enclosed area to keep her from danger.

God doesn't put up physical fences in our lives. Instead, He tells us in the Scriptures about the narrow and wide gates. Matthew 7:13-14 says, "Enter through the narrow gate; for wide is the gate and broad is the road that leads to destruction, and many enter through it. But small is the gate and narrow the road that leads to life, and only a few find it." Unlike Cassy, we do not have a physical boundary marker to keep us from unsafe, rough, or creepy paths; instead, we are warned of the dangers of choosing the wrong path and encouraged to choose the right one.

Just like Cassy, we can also get distracted by something or someone and venture onto a dangerous pathway. There have been many times in my life that I chose to go down a road I knew was not in line with what The Lord would have me do. Times like these are when I feel distant from Him, or lost, in a sense. It is only after I confess, honestly ask forgiveness, and return to Him, that I can continue on the right path.

If Cassy were to get hurt or lost, I would be overwhelmed by sadness, because she is very precious to me. Not surprisingly though, we are even *more* precious to our Master than our beloved pups are to us. "Are not two sparrows sold for a penny? Yet not one of them will fall to the ground outside your Father's care" (Matthew 10:29). "So don't be afraid; you are worth more than many sparrows." (Matthew 10:31). He invites us and encourages us to travel the right road of life, *the narrow road*, because He loves us and wants to keep us secure. His word is like an invisible fence for us to live by.

I love opening up the back door and enthusiastically shouting, "OK Scoopy, go play." Off she runs, like an excited child getting ready to sit on Santa's lap. Thump, thump, thump, down the steps and onto the deck she goes. She stops, looks up at me for approval, and then continues on toward the open grassy yard like a free spirit. She loves to run, chase birds and bark her head off, all in the protected confines of our newly fenced yard.

Just like Cassy, I love the freedom I have in my relationship with the Lord. I must remember, like her, to stop, look to my Master for approval and then continue in the way of righteousness knowing that He will keep me as the apple of His eye and will hide me in the shadow of His wings (Psalm 17:8).

Chapter 23: Don't Fence Me In

Chapter 24

The Little Dog Who Could

Did you ever wonder if perseverance is a gift? Let's face it; some of us persist in trying to achieve our intended goal, and others just give up even before attempting often enough to determine if they could succeed. I recently learned of a senior, overweight dog named Nugget who persevered with extraordinary persistence and gutsiness.

Nugget was owned by Sophie and her husband John. Although both were close to Nugget, John was the one Nugget loved most, spent the greatest time with, and he was Nugget's true master. After 12 years of being a part of Nugget's life, John passed away from a terminal illness.

Sophie told me that after her husband died, Nugget was clearly depressed. Her head was no longer held high; her brown eyes were large, somber and sorrowful looking. Her countenance was distinctly troubled and low spirited. She would go from room to room looking for her master, John. She wandered aimlessly around, whining, as if she were saying, "Where are you? I miss you."

Although an active and loved member of the family, certain areas of the house were off-limits to Nugget. A gate was used to block her from gaining access to her master's bedroom.

Nugget never attempted to scale the gate because she learned early on as a pup that her boundary line, defined by the gate, precluded her from the bedroom. However, after the death of her master, Nugget felt compelled to somehow try and get closer to the room that had always been inaccessible to her.

Nugget would lie next to the gate and peer through the rails into the dimly lit bedroom which was now only occupied by Sophie (a sweet elderly lady who was understandably heartbroken herself).

Due to advanced age and obesity, Nugget had severe hip problems and could hardly walk, much less climb or jump. Getting over the bedroom gate would have been all but impossible for her.

Sophie told me that one night she was awakened from a sound sleep when something or someone had startled her. She wasn't sure if she was dreaming or not. The nightlight near her bed was casting a soft glow, and the hum of the ceiling fan drowned out the chirping of the crickets that occupied her heavily wooded backyard. Everything seemed fine, but there was an unfamiliar faint sound that she could hear when she listened attentively.

Sophie was a little frightened initially, but couldn't ignore what sounded like someone breathing in her bedroom. As she lay tensely in her bed, she wondered why Nugget did not bark or alert her in some way to the possibility that something was wrong. She bravely decided to get up and investigate, and at the same time, check on Nugget. She did so, carefully feeling her way along the bed with her hands.

As she gingerly inched toward the gate that separated her bedroom from the hall, she gasped as she almost tripped over something large, warm, and furry lying on the floor. It was Nugget! Sophie was bewildered. She staggered unsteadily in an attempt to firmly balance herself, wondering how Nugget could have possibly gotten there. After all, Nugget could not have climbed over the gate, or had she? Indeed, Nugget was sleeping on the floor that night near the side of the bed where Sophie's husband would have slept.

The following night, Sophie witnessed Nugget, once again, try numerous times to get over the gate until she succeeded, and then went right into the bedroom to sleep. Perhaps it was to protect Sophie or just to be nearer to her master's scent. Something compelled Nugget to climb over the gate even after several failed attempts. She did not give up; she persevered. She did so with honor, grace, and gutsiness.

The Random House dictionary aptly defines perseverance as a "steady persistence in a course of action, a purpose, a state, etc., especially in spite of difficulties, obstacles or discouragement."

Nugget's tenacity reminds me of the small blue engine in the tale, *The Little Engine Who Could*, written by Arnold Munk in the early 1950s. The small engine succeeds in pulling a train over the mountain while repeating the mantra "I think I can, I think I can," and overcomes a seemingly impossible task. Nugget also succeeded in overcoming the very obstacle that blocked her for so many years from being closer to her master. Now she sleeps every night protecting, guiding, and honoring Sophie.

Hebrews 12:1-2 says, "Let us run with perseverance the race marked out for us, fixing our eyes on Jesus, [Our Master] the pioneer perfecter of faith. For the joy set before him, He endured the cross."

For twelve years, Nugget was content to make her bed in a part of the house that was made accessible to her. She never challenged the gate. It was not her goal to make her bed in her master's room until he passed away. However, after he did, Nugget persisted with a course of action in spite of her difficulties.

Like Nugget, we are encouraged to also press on toward the goal to win the prize for which God has called us heavenward in Christ Jesus (Philippians 3:14). Let's persevere with honor, grace, and gutsiness. God promises us, if we do not get weary in doing good, we will reap a harvest if we do not give up (Galatians 6:9).

Chapter 25

The Tree, The Lights, The Baby

It was early fall, in the crisp month of September, that our new life as pet owners began. Cassy was only eleven weeks old when we brought her into our home. The first few weeks of training were challenging and stressful, (as we tried to learn how to train our puppy, being the novice pet owners that we were) but, at the same time, wonderfully memorable. Time seemed to fly by quickly, and we knew the challenges of puppyhood would soon be behind us. We wanted to enjoy every moment.

Cassy was still a rambunctious little puppy in December of that same year when we celebrated Christmas. I wondered how she would behave with all the temptations of the glitter and glamour of the season. For several weeks, prior to and after the holidays, we had decorations, lights, mistletoe, and boughs of Holly that were now inside of our home that previously had not been there.

We placed our freshly cut Christmas tree in the corner of the family room between the kitchen and living room. The fresh pine scent filled our entire house. Cassy's little senses were overloaded both visually and perceptually. She watched with wonder as we dressed the tree with glittering lights, shimmering garland, and an array of ornaments that we collected over many years. Many of these ornaments resembled her toys, especially those made of cloth or other soft fabric. The presents were carefully wrapped and neatly tied with ribbon and bows. They circled the base of the tree, adding to its already alluring appeal to this rather curious pup.

In the center of the myriad of beautifully wrapped packages, was the Nativity, simple in appearance, and humbly representative of the first Christmas, the birth of Jesus, the Savior of the world. As we placed the last ornament on the top branch, we gazed at our tree with delight and excitement; however, I could not help but wonder if our new pup would respect our masterpiece like we did.

Over the next several days following the trimming of the tree, I was pleasantly surprised to see that Cassy apparently had very little interest in this great, green, fragrant, pine timber now occupying our family room. She did not snatch any ornaments or maliciously tear the paper or ribbons off the gifts. She hardly seemed to notice them.

Would she behave the same way if she was left alone in the house with this alluringly large, pine tree with all of its decorations and embellishments? Would I come home to find unwrapped presents strewn across the floor with paper, bows and tape everywhere? Would we have to visit Dr. Jennifer to have Cassy assessed for eating a foreign object that a curious little pup should not have consumed? Luckily, Cassy did none of the above. She did; however, "steal Jesus." She didn't bother Mary, Joseph, or any other part of the crèche, but she carefully and gently used her mouth to lift baby Jesus up out of His tiny bed.

We discovered that she would hide Him in another part of the room. Perhaps it was the size of the small linen wrapped baby doll that was so similarly close to one of her toys. Whatever the reason, she would only take Jesus from the crèche; not any of the other figurines, presents, ornaments or other decorations. We finally decided to remove the baby from its little straw lined manger, and put it out of Cassy's reach, so she wouldn't break it.

Cassy's antics, although quite amusing, made me realize how many people concentrate on the tree, the lights, and the presents instead of focusing on the One whom we are celebrating. Luke 2:11-12 says, "Today in the town of David, a Savior has been born to you; He is the Messiah, the Lord... You will find a baby wrapped in clothes lying in a manger." Although Jesus entered the world as a baby, He did not stay asleep in the manger. He came to fulfill the promise given to the prophet Isaiah. "Therefore, the Lord Himself will give you a sign; the virgin will be with child and will give birth to a son, and will call Him Immanuel [God with us]" (Isaiah 7:14). He came to redeem us, save us and to give us eternal life. Just looking at Jesus under the tree is not enough. We must receive, (take) Him into our heart and accept His gift of salvation.

Cassy took Jesus from the crèche for her own pleasure. However, we need to *take* Jesus for our eternal salvation. Cassy selfishly hid Him. We should share Him with all mankind. That is the Gospel, the good news.

Let's honor Him not only at Christmas time, but every day throughout the year. Let's not focus on the tree, the lights, and the presents only. Let's focus on the Baby. Let's "take Him from under the tree" and hide Him in our hearts.

Chapter 26

Say What!

Cassy spends a lot of time sleeping. When she eats, she eats a lot. When she plays, she plays a lot, but when she sleeps, she *really* sleeps a lot. Cassy gives new meaning to the saying, "dog day afternoons," although, in her case, she sleeps most of the morning. The only thing she doesn't do is talk a lot. In fact, Cassy does not talk at all; she never has and never will.

It is incredible to think that our precious pets spend so much time with us and many live very long lives, but they never speak. Now I am not saying they don't communicate; they actually do, just not with words.

I can always tell when Cassy wants to play. She will get her favorite blue ball, hold it between her upper and lower jaws while her tail is wagging relentlessly back and forth like a motorized fan. She will come within inches of me, very close to my feet, and make squealing, throaty, playful growling sounds. Her backside is up in the air while her front paws and chest are lower to the ground. Her body language speaks volumes as she expresses clearly to me "come on, let's have some fun!"

If I choose to participate in her invitation to play, and throw her ball, she will run to retrieve it, pick it up again and happily return to me ready for round two, three and four. This game will continue until I call a time out or game over. If I throw her ball, and it rolls under the coffee table or couch, she will stare into the blank space where she saw the ball roll and moan as if saying, "help, I can't get my ball." Her playful, excited temperament is once again evidenced by her tail wagging faster than a flag in the wind. I understand her language because she is my dog. I know her very well.

Did you know that the average woman speaks approximately 20,000 words per day, and the average man speaks roughly 7,000 words per day? The majority of both sexes, unless they are mute, communicate verbally, most of the time. Dogs, however, communicate eloquently with their tails, but also with growling, moaning, barking, and even with their bodies by jumping and/or circling around. I am sure there are many other forms of dog language that I have not listed. Dogs usually know what they want and they tell us without ever speaking one single word.

Ephesians 4:29 instructs us to guard what we say. "Do not let any unwholesome talk come out of your mouths, but only what is helpful for building others up according to their needs, that it may benefit those who listen." Interestingly, we use our tongues to help us properly form our words, but our thoughts are first conceived in our minds. Our hearts need to be pure in order for our mind to produce pleasant thoughts that are then communicated verbally. Our tongues can make words that will be either a blessing or a curse to the recipient of those words.

Fire, in the same way, can be good (giving us warmth and light) or destructive (burning us, our homes or nature) if it gets out of control. James 3:5-6 warns, the tongue is a small part of the body, but it makes great boasts. Consider what a great forest is set on fire by a small spark. The tongue is also a fire ... "And yes. That fire can cause much damage.

No matter what kind of day Cassy is having, whether she is basking in the sun, sleeping in her bed (dreaming of her blue ball) or peering out the window hoping to go outside and run like the wind, her body language almost always communicates unconditional happiness.

Her reaction to just seeing me return home from a short trip to my neighborhood grocery mart evokes delight and enthusiasm in her and blesses me in return. She never *speaks* angrily toward me. I have never witnessed expressions of bitterness, displeasure, or vexation in her. Instead, I see her stubby little wagging tail saying, "I love you; you're the greatest, most beautiful person in the whole wide world."

We can all learn from our four-legged friends to use our tongues the way they use their tails. We also can bless one another, praise our friends and loved ones, and speak words of unconditional affirmation, to those closest to us. Let's practice the art of communicating what is in our hearts before speaking what is on our minds.

James 1:19 says, "Everyone should be quick to listen, slow to speak and slow to become angry."

Proverbs 18:4 says, "The words of the mouth are deep waters, but the fountain of wisdom is a rushing stream."

Chapter 27

Danny Boy

Seven weeks after starting his first year of medical school, our son Michael visited an animal shelter in Greenville, NC. He went there hoping to rescue *the one* who would become his best friend; a companion "who sticks closer than a brother."

There were many candidates to choose from that were waiting to find their forever home and become "the lucky dog of the day." After he carefully surveyed the already overcrowded rescue center, Mike spotted an underweight, lanky black lab mix, who was easily excitable, but at the same time, shy.

The shelter workers encouraged Mike to go out back into the fenced area where he and this potential adoptee could get to know each other better. The two of them ran around a bit, played fetch with a ball, and began to bond with each other rather quickly.

Out of all the many prospective dogs, this boy won the affection of Mike's heart. He then sat on the ground in the grassy field behind the shelter and called his new buddy to his side. As the dog approached him, he was leaping with excitement, and his tail was wagging back and forth. He then obediently came to Mike's side and immediately sat down while keeping his warm, dark, blackish-brown eyes fixed on my son. This dog had best friend qualities written all over him and Mike was certain that Danny, the name given to him by Mike, was destined to be his.

Mike had to work very hard to gain Danny's trust and become Danny's leader. When Mike was with him, Danny was eager and ready to please his master. He loved playing and running with Mike, and was equally content just to lie down next to him, as long as they were together. In fact, Danny Boy (affectionately known as DB) did not want to be left alone or abandoned ever again. He didn't like being separated from his master. He wanted the assurance that Mike would come home at the end of each day.

Danny suffered from extreme separation anxiety every time he was left alone. His fretful behavior caused him to destroy a lot of Mike's personal property. When Danny acted out and shredded Mike's large, expensive textbook, it was a sure sign that separation from his master caused him stress. He was so upset, and it showed up in the bits and pieces of text strewn all over the apartment floor. He was not about to lay around and sleep like a dog all day until Mike came home. He was clearly not happy. Of course, Mike was going to return at the end of the day, but Danny didn't understand that yet. He only knew that, at the present moment, his master was not there.

One particular day, when Mike was getting ready to leave his apartment, he tried to console Danny and affectionately told him he would return in a few hours. Although Danny couldn't understand, Mike was hoping he could help ease Danny's anxiety with words of affirmation.

He put Danny in his crate, which not only provided a safe haven for him, but it also helped to protect Mike's things from being destroyed. He was so upset when Mike left home to go to class, that he began to whine and bark wildly and loudly.

His anxiety quickly heightened, and he started to use the strength of his body to move the crate erratically. After many attempts to free himself, he was finally able to force his slender black body through a small opening between the metal bars.

When he broke out of the crate; however, he injured himself in the process. Separation from his master was terrible for Danny and even caused him to become physically distraught. His agitated fit from the apprehension of being left alone resulted in a laceration to his head.

Like Danny, all of us need the assurance, from time to time, that we will not be abandoned and left alone. In Hebrews 13:5, we read, "Never will I leave you; never will I forsake you." God never deserts His children and He never breaks a promise. I take comfort in knowing that my Master is always with me.

Even Jesus felt alone and abandoned when His disciples fell asleep in the Garden of Gethsemane while He was agonizing in prayer (Matthew 26:36-46). These guys were His friends, His brothers, and yet, when He needed them, they were asleep. Again, the Scriptures record for us that Jesus, when nailed to the cross, felt the intense emotional pain from being separated from God, The Father. The Scriptures tell us that "He cried out, My God, My God; why have you forsaken me" (Matthew 27:46)? Thanks to the resurrection, Jesus will never again be separated from His Father and is with Him now and forever.

Although Mike reassured Danny countless times that he was going to return, it took many months for trust to be established between them. There was nothing Mike could do to break Danny of the distressing state he would work himself into other than consistency and discipline. Eventually, after many attempts to calm this terrified dog, Mike gained Danny's trust.

Our Master wants our trust too, and His promises to us are even more trustworthy than Mike's to Danny. We have the Holy Spirit who is always with us. His promise to never leave or forsake us is an eternal promise, and nothing can separate from Him, those who are His. In Matthew 28:20, we read the most comforting words that Jesus Himself spoke, which brought peace to those in His presence at that time and for us today, "And surely I am with you always, even to the very end of the age."

Chapter 27: Danny Boy

Chapter 28

Hide and Seek

Occasionally Cassy gets rewarded with a new chew stick or cookie treat. She eagerly accepts it as she gingerly picks it up with her mouth and firmly holds it between her jaws. She then journeys from room to room with her tail wagging, making low pitched, whimpering sounds, searching, and sniffing for a place to hide it. She will hoard her treat, sometimes for days before chewing on it or eating it up. She gets very possessive and will even attempt to bury the precious, crunchy morsel in the corner of a room or behind an open door. It is as if burying it gives her a sense of ownership of the treat and then she (and only she) gets the prize when she retrieves it. In the end, she is always the winner because she's the only one who knows where it is hidden.

Her antics are quite humorous, and watching her lurk around eyeing up a potential hiding spot can be very entertaining. She will sneak quietly into a room like a cat on the prowl as it hunts for its prey. She will then frantically use her front paws to dig up an invisible habitat for her precious possession. Her jet black, wet nose is on sensory overload as it twitches from side to side and, in true Sherlockian fashion, she will sniff out the perfect location to hide her new indulgence. Sometimes she will sit and stare, as if watching paint dry, at the newly prepared burial spot for quite some time before dropping the treat into it from her mouth. However, I never reprimand her for this behavior, or try to teach her to be less possessive. After all, she is a dog and this is in her nature.

As I think about Cassy's affinity with her treats, I can't help but wonder about my nature and if my attachments to some things cause me to be inappropriately possessive. How much value do I place on my worldly stuff? What are the desires of my heart? Do I place enough value on my identity as a Christian?

In Psalm 119:11 we read, "I have hidden your word in my heart that I might not sin against you." These are the words of King David which I believe reveal his nature and his passion. He was possessive, not for things, but for God and God's word. Throughout the Psalms, we read where David is seeking the Lord, and asking to be hidden, not *from* God, but *in* God. Psalm 17:8 says, "Keep me as the apple of your eye; Hide me in the shadow of Your wings."

Cassy gets consistent correction and discipline from me and my husband Joe. She is a wonderful little pet, and we know that this will help keep her that way. If she was left to her own instinctive behavior, she undoubtedly would fulfill her desire to do things that would not be acceptable to us. I can almost see her now ripping through the kitchen trash in search of leftover chicken bones, filling her tummy with scraps of gourmet garbage. Perhaps, she might also choose to meander into our closet and steal my new fleece lined slippers. I'm sure she would have a grand time de-fleecing them, or at the very least, tearing them apart. Luckily, Cassy does not do these things because we have taught her that certain behaviors are not pleasing to us. In spite of how good she is though, she will continue to instinctively behave like a terrier and bury her toys and treats. She will never seek after God because she is a dog. She is driven only to exercise her natural desires while also seeking to please me and Joe.

Unlike Cassy's behavior, I do not want to only exercise my natural desires; I also want to fulfill my spiritual life by *burying* myself in Him and His word. As a Christian, I instinctively want to know God better, and like King David, I want to "hide His word in my heart." I must first start by preparing a suitable home for God's word. Like the psalmist, I must ask the Lord for His help. "Search me, God, and know my heart; test me, and know my anxious thoughts. See if there is any offensive way in me, and lead me in the way everlasting" (Psalm 139:23-24).

Cassy always rewards herself by eating her treat, her prized possession, after hiding it in her secret place. She will excavate her treasure and feast happily on the tasty morsel. God tells us that His word is food for us. "Man shall not live on bread alone, but on every word that comes from the mouth of God" (Matthew 4:4).

As I hide myself in Him, and He in me, I can satisfy my spiritual hunger and *eat* daily from the banquet table of His promises and His word.

Chapter 29

Just One Touch

I can remember a time, prior to my ownership of Cassy, when I thought, *I will never be that person who alters their plans around a pet's schedule.* I assumed that if folks owned a pet, that someone (anyone), could let them out when they needed to go. Well, I am that person; I admit it. I will carefully map out my day or evening with the help of my interactive mapping app that not only details the best route, but also estimates departure and arrival times. Now I can plan with precision around Cassy's schedule.

Like me, have you ever wondered what your pet does when home, alone? Whenever we are getting ready to leave the house, I begin to feel a tinge of guilt because Cassy can't always go where we go. It is amazing to me that she seems to understand that we are leaving as she studies our every move with her dark chocolate colored brown eyes. Because Joe and I are creatures of habit, there are obvious cues in our routine that tip her off to our impending departure.

For instance, she knows that I usually blow dry my hair, brush my teeth, and put on lipstick before heading out the door. Joe will typically wait to put on a freshly ironed shirt and will also stop to brush up before he heads out. Cassy will sit somberly, watching us rush around, but will jump up excitedly on all four paws as we begin our exit toward the door. She gets in ready mode as if she is preparing to come with us. However, most of the time we say goodbye to her, and leave.

If only I were a fly on the wall, then I could see what she does when she's home alone. Does she curl up in her very own bed? Does she play hide and seek with her blue ball? Perhaps she just sleeps for hours on my bed or in the sunny spot on the front staircase steps. In my perfect world, she is as content as a cloudless spring day.

I probably will never know exactly what she does or doesn't do when home alone. One thing I do know though, when we return, Cassy is one happy pup. She celebrates our homecoming with enthusiastic squealing, running in circles, tail wagging, and lots of kisses. Her misery of being alone is dramatically transformed as we enter the house. Cassy's great fortune of having her two-favorite people return ignites her spirit with playfulness and delight.

Following the glorious reception, Cassy will again assume her role as a follower of both Joe and me. As we walk through the house, she will trail us by harmonizing in our steps as if tethered to our ankles by an imaginary line. Whether we are sitting at the computer, watching TV, reading, or lying in bed, Cassy has to be touching us. Sometimes her head will be on my lap while her back paws are on Joe's lap at the same time.

She appears content and comfortable by being able to *feel* her masters' presence. It is not enough for her to be near us; she must be touching us. This physical contact relaxes her, like a child in the arms of her parent, and gives her a sense of imperturbable peace.

Cassy's need for touch reminds me of the lady who was healed by "… just the touch of the Lord's garment" (Matthew 9:21-22).

In Matthew 14:36 we read that "… all who touched Him were healed." What do you think it would be like to place your hand or head on Jesus? To curl up next to Him and sleep peacefully, unmoved, unruffled, and undisturbed even during times of chaos, sickness, or fear. Do we remember His precious words in Matthew 11:28? "Come to me, all you who are weary and burdened, and I will give you rest."

Joe and I can give Cassy all the physical contact, security, and comfort she desires, as long as we are in her presence. In our absence, she does not have access to these pleasurable, peaceful feelings.

Unlike Cassy, we, God's children, have access to Him, through Jesus, because of the Holy Spirit. Thankfully, Jesus did not leave us alone and without the security, comfort and peace that was known by those who were in physical contact with Him. After His departure from earth to heaven, He sent the comforter, the Holy Spirit, to be with us during His time of physical absence from this world. We read in Matthew 28:20, Jesus' gracious promise, "and surely I am with you always, to the very end of the age." Early on in the Old Testament, the prophet Isaiah tells us, "the virgin will be with child and will give birth to a son; they will call Him Immanuel, which means, God is with us."

Today we can still take hold of His garment by taking hold of Him, His word and His promises. We can rest in the eternal security, which is found only in Him. Cassy does not have access to her master's spirit in our physical absence, but we have access to our Master's spirit in His physical absence. Today I will remember that despite the uncertainty of this world, I can trust unwaveringly in Jesus. Just like the lyrics of the song, "I've got Peace Like a River in my soul," I can rest in Him. Just one touch (by Him) is all it takes.

Chapter 30

Stretch Up

A lot of people are good at stretching their imaginations or their monthly budgets. Cassy is good at limbering up by stretching her body, especially every tendon and ligament in her front and back paws. She does this each morning when she wakes. As she stretches out like the green colored rubber character Gumby, you can audibly hear her joints crackle like embers popping from a fire while she does the army crawl across the bedroom carpet. She then reaches forward with her front paws while she drags her stiffened, fully extended back paws, like a caboose of a train. Perhaps her body gets a little lethargic from sleeping for hours curled up in a ball, and this daily exercise ritual prepares her for running and playing.

When Cassy stretches each morning, it reminds me that I need to do the same, especially as it relates to my relationship with the Lord. I want to be careful not to get lazy with my prayer time or apathetic about my devotions. Complacency can cause me, and other believers like me to stop exercising our faith. The bumps and valleys of life are often the very things that stretch us and cause us to grow in our relationship with God. Adversity on this side of Heaven is a part of life for every believer. We are reminded in the Gospel of John 16:33, "In this world you will have trouble. But take heart! I have overcome the world." We must be attentive, diligent, and careful each day to maintain our spiritual health, so we will be fit when we need to exercise our faith. We ought to stretch our hands and hearts toward Heaven.

Perhaps Cassy feels good after stretching her furry cream-colored extremities across the soft plush bedroom carpet. Maybe this daily routine helps to keep her physically sound, fit as a fiddle and prepares her for wakefulness. However, one thing it will not do, is strengthen her spirit, or cause her to grow. It is merely a behavioral practice that is common in many breeds.

On the other hand, we will not grow unless we are stretched. James 1:2-3 says, "Consider it pure joy, my brothers and sisters, whenever you face trials of many kinds, because you know that the testing of your faith produces perseverance." Although few people, if any, choose or ask for trials in their lives, the stress and tension produced from them usually results in a positive outcome. Those who persevere under the weight of life's challenges will be like a diamond, which until exposed to extreme pressure over time, was only a hunk of coal. When the heat gets turned up and the blue skies of life turn gray, we can trust in God's word. Philippians 4:7 says, "And the peace of God, which surpasses all understanding, will guard your hearts and minds through Christ Jesus."

As our faith continues to be tested daily, our spiritual muscles will strengthen when we remain focused on Him. "It is God who arms me with strength and keeps my way secure" (2 Samuel 22:33).

Cassy will continue to stretch out her limbs, neck, and torso every morning to get ready for the activities of each day. I plan to continue exercising my faith and feeding my spirit with the daily bread of His word. This, in addition to "putting on the full armor of God," as we are instructed in Ephesians 6:10-18, will enable me to be ready for the day ahead.

Chapter 30: Stretch Up

Chapter 31

Joy in the Suffering

Prior to becoming a dog owner, I was profoundly aware that part of my responsibility to our pet would be to have her routinely checked by a veterinarian to ensure good health and well-being. I assumed that a nutritious diet, adequate exercise, and a safe protective environment would guarantee a long hearty life for her.

As I looked over my list of good dog parenting tips, I was confident that I could check off many, if not all, of the ingenious ideas I had planned to carry out in order to keep Cassy healthy. Although my intentions and efforts proved most successful for her first 18 months of life, something in her typically happy disposition started changing as she neared two years of age.

I was puzzled because at that age, our girl should not be slowing down. Because of that I began to fear that maybe something was wrong with our precious pup. Over the course of several weeks, she would not bear weight on her left hind paw. Her running was interrupted mid-stride, and she was beginning to show signs of extreme discomfort even with walking. She never complained, nevertheless. There was no moaning, groaning, or yelping; however, we knew she was hurting due to her lack of desire to run and greet us as she previously had.

I admit, I was fearful, and prayed that she would be okay. After all, the Lord knew she was (and still is) near and dear to my heart.

Her little 14-pound body was carefully examined, poked, prodded, and probed by Dr. Jennifer, Cassy's veterinarian. I intensely watched the doctor with concern, and I carefully studied her every move. I then found myself staring anxiously into her face, scrutinizing closely, watching her facial expressions and countenance, as she methodically continued to examine Cassy with extreme detail.

My spirit was strong, but my flesh was weakening as I began to feel uncertain about the outcome of the exam. X-rays were ordered and performed, at last revealing the nature of Cassy's debilitating problem. Our vet referred us to an orthopedic surgeon for a consultation to learn about and discuss her diagnosis, patellar luxation.

Patellar luxation occurs when the dog's kneecap (patella) is dislocated from its normal anatomic position in the groove of the thigh bone (femur). Surgical intervention would be required to repair this congenital defect and give Cassy her active life back.

On March 18, 2010, Dr. Gary, the orthopedic specialist, performed the necessary surgery on Cassy's left leg. Following the surgery, we were instructed to keep her quiet during the six-week post-op phase. No up and down steps, no running in the yard or jumping up onto furniture. The gates in the house went up, and the recovery period began. Cassy did awesome.

Her one-week follow-up appointment showed excellent results. Cassy was coming along just fine. Prior to seeing Dr. Gary that day, we sat in the waiting area with other pet parents and their pets.

One thing that impressed me as we waited was how Cassy and the other dogs we saw at the animal hospital responded not only to the stress of being there, but also to the surgery. I didn't hear crying or whining. There were no complaints, or bitter barks, or displays of "why me?" attitudes. Instead, I witnessed wagging tails, happy sounds and looks of gratitude.

We met Rocky, a German Shepard, who had a rare cancer involving his eyes and sinuses. He sat confidently, upright, and proudly at his master's side just delighted to be cared for by his loving owners.

Cassy had been wearing an E-collar, short for Elizabethan collar, which encircled her head to prevent her from licking her surgical site and potentially tearing out her sutures. She wasn't thrilled with this obtrusive, yet necessary apparatus, but nonetheless, she never complained. However, throughout the six weeks of wearing it, she would shake her head back and forth like a flag in the wind attempting to free herself from this circular head vice. Thankfully, her attempts proved futile.

People can learn so much from their four-legged pets. How do we respond to the stress and discomfort of surgery, illness, and hospitalization? Do we wag our tails and express joy and gratitude in spite of our situation? Certainly, there are circumstances that go beyond what one could bear, but many times I believe we need to try and see the silver lining through the dark storm clouds of life. Romans 8:18 says, "I consider that our present sufferings are not worth comparing with the glory that will be revealed in us".

The apostle Paul suffered greatly in his time on earth and Paul even states in his own words, "I have great sorrow and unceasing anguish in my heart" (Romans 9:2). His response is recorded in Romans 15:13, "May the God of hope fill you with all joy and peace as you trust in Him, so that you may overflow with hope by the power of the Holy Spirit."

Our brave little Cassy and Rocky, the German shepherd, seem to have risen above their circumstances when they were going through obvious uncomfortable situations. I wonder if part of their determination to get well quickly was due to focusing less on their problems and more on their masters. I will never know the answer to this since they are dogs and can't tell us, but maybe I am on to something.

On the other hand, we can look confidently to the Scriptures that will always exhort us to keep our focus on our Master, whether in times of plenty or want, vibrant health or sickness, and periods of joy or suffering. Philippians 4:11 says, "I am not saying this because I am in need, for I have learned to be content whatever the circumstances."

Chapter 31: Joy in the Suffering

Chapter 32

Shakin' Like a Leaf

Cassy has a heightened sensitivity to certain smells and sounds that many times aren't normally heard or detected by anyone but her. It is not unusual to observe her generally sweet and confident countenance change quickly to vigilant and wide-eyed, especially when she perceives stimuli that others don't see, hear, or smell.

When in high alert, she will bolt up the stairs to the second-floor bathroom to hide. She probably chooses that room because it is between two bedrooms and has no windows. It is usually dark, due to no natural light, and because of its small size, she most likely feels safe from outside elements. She will sit, ears fixed upright like antennas, reaching to hear even the most inaudible sounds. It is as if she has radar and knows intuitively that something is not right.

She responds attentively to the warning signs that to her are signaling danger. Almost predictably, after several minutes I will faintly hear a distant rumble of thunder or a gush of violent wind wrapping its forceful arms around the outside of our house. Cassy will wait it out upstairs in the small bathroom until she senses the *all clear*. Her response to the eminent sights and sounds of an approaching storm typically evokes such terror in her that she will tremble and shake like a leaf. Relaxation and calm usually return to her at the conclusion of the unsettling event.

God has given countless warning signs to His people throughout history. He spoke to many Old Testament prophets commanding them to warn the people of that time about things yet to come.

Do you remember the storied account of Noah when he was warned by God of the impending great destruction God was going to send to the earth through a flood? Noah tried to warn the known world of that time, but other than his family, no one heeded the message.

Noah obediently responded by building an ark when there was not even a cloud in sight, and his family was spared the awful consequences of defiance toward God.

Jesus has graciously warned the world, that in order to inherit the kingdom of heaven, one must believe in Him, and accept His death as a sacrifice for our sin, or suffer a terrible eternity without Him.

We are also warned throughout the Scriptures that Jesus will return to earth someday and will take His bride (us) to Himself, if we have obediently responded to His invitation. Many listeners in Jesus' day responded willingly and appropriately to His warning and followed Him. Yet, there were others who did not heed the signs that were clearly evident in His ministry, such as the prophesy found in Isaiah 7:14, "Therefore, the Lord Himself will give you a sign; the virgin will conceive and give birth to a son, and will call Him Immanuel." Isaiah's prophecy was fulfilled and is recorded in Matthew 1:18-23.

Just as the saints of old were warned that Jesus would come to earth when He did, as a baby in Bethlehem, so He will return to earth again as a conquering King as we are told in Hebrews 10:37. "For, in just a very little while, He who is coming will come and will not delay."

In Revelation 1:7-8 we read, "Look, He is coming with the clouds and every eye will see Him, even those who pierced Him; and all the peoples on earth will mourn because of Him. So shall it be! Amen. 'I am the Alpha and the Omega,' says the Lord God, 'who is, and who was and who is to come, the Almighty.'"

When Cassy shakes like a leaf from external forces, I do not coddle her. Coddling may possibly heighten her fear. Instead, I reward her after she settles down by taking her for a walk or speaking lovingly toward her. My goal is not to reinforce the fear, but instead, bolster her quiet trust in her master.

I believe our reward will be immeasurably great when we trust our Master and obey His teaching. Eternal security in Heaven and seeing Jesus face to face are just two of the countless rewards we will get to enjoy. Listen for God's warnings. They will be eternally worthy and richly rewarded.

Chapter 33

Love Never Fails

During my career days when working as a registered nurse, one of my coworkers, Joan, made a comment that, at the time, seemed absurd and outrageous to me. She blatantly stated that she liked dogs more than people.

Now this was BC (before Cassy); therefore, I was shocked, to say the least, to hear her say this, especially aloud. After all, aren't we supposed to keep these thoughts private, hushed and unspoken?

As I pondered her puzzling conversation stopper, I had to reel myself back to the Joan I had known and worked alongside for many years. She was a great person: a true humanitarian, wonderful nurse, and friend. Her hair-raising statement just didn't make sense.

My conclusion (which by the way, was confirmed by Joan) was not that she didn't like people; it's simply that she liked the qualities that dogs naturally exhibit and demonstrate. Of course, many people possess these same qualities; they just don't always demonstrate them. It is more of a choice with people to exercise unconditional love, whereas expressing unconditional love seems to be instinctive and natural to dogs.

In 1984, the Wendy's Burger Restaurant chain coined the phrase, "Where's the Beef?" as part of their advertising campaign. Many in our culture today ask, "Where's the Love?"

Turn on the news and one would be more inclined to ask, "Why so much hate?" Is it actually possible to love others unconditionally, especially those who are unlovely? Paul, the author of the book of Romans, says it is possible. "If your enemy is hungry, feed him; if he is thirsty, give him something to drink" (Romans 12:20). Notice Paul doesn't list any conditions. We are just instructed to give to whomever is in need, even our enemies.

Love for others is demonstrated in very tangible ways, on a daily basis, by many individuals, and by various missionary organizations. One worth mentioning is Samaritan's Purse, which has provided 135 million gift filled shoe boxes to children in more than 150 countries since 1993 through the Operation Christmas Child project. (2016 Fact Sheet, Operation Christmas Child.)

The Bible uses several different Greek words for love. The two used most frequently are Phileo and Agape. I believe that since love is the most distinctive character of the Christian life, as modeled to us by Jesus, God wants us to have a deeper, and greater understanding of what it means to love others.

The definition of phileo is to treat affectionately or kindly, to welcome, befriend. It is also known as brotherly love. Agape speaks of the most powerful kind of love. It is more than a feeling, rather an act of the will. This is the love that God has toward us, His children.

Perhaps it is because she is an avid dog lover that Joan is able to see the attributes in dogs that compel her to speak so highly of these four-legged creatures.

If you own a dog now or ever have in the past, you are probably familiar with their loyalty, devotion and unparalleled love that are completely independent of any conditions, especially for their owners and family members. It's just part of who they are. Of course, there are always exceptions, but most well-cared-for animals respectfully honor their masters.

For those of us who are children of God, we have His very Spirit dwelling in our hearts which enables us to love as He loves. "For the fruit of the Spirit is love..." (Galatians 5:22).

We can and should extend love toward others often. Since, as I mentioned earlier, love is the distinctive characteristic of the Christian life, we will be known by the fruit we bear. (Matthew 7:20) Unlike dogs, who love instinctively, we must choose to love.

As I choose to love others as Jesus loves me, I promise not to lick anyone's face, like Cassy does, but I will smile, hold someone's hand, give a hug, or just wag my tail (so to speak), even if they don't deserve it.

"Love is patient, love is kind. It does not envy, it does not boast, it is not proud. It does not dishonor others, it is not self-seeking, it is not easily angered, it keeps no record of wrongs. Love does not delight in evil but rejoices with the truth. It always protects, always trusts, always hopes, always perseveres. Love never fails" (1 Corinthians 13:4-8). Now this sums up what Love truly is.

Chapter 34

Will You Be My Friend?

When I was a young girl, I loved watching "I Love Lucy," which to this day, still makes me laugh hysterically. Now I know this really dates me, but I truly enjoy many of the classic shows from back in the day.

One episode I recall from this classic TV era was "Lucy's Last Birthday." It seemed as though everyone, her husband, family, and friends, had forgotten her birthday. She was depressed and was wandering around town when she met up with "Friends of the Friendless," who were a mob of unhappy people united together in a park. Apparently, they found solidarity in each other, and before you knew it, Lucy, because of her presumption that she was forgotten on her birthday, joined the ranks of this motley crew.

Of course, this episode, and every other, ended well, leaving its viewers happy. Lucy's sadness at the start of the "Lucy's Last Birthday" episode didn't last very long. Predictably, she was not forgotten and a surprise celebration was planned by all that loved her.

Fortunately, I do not ever remember feeling deprived in my relationships with others.

I married my childhood sweetheart, and we will celebrate 36 years together in May 2017.

God has blessed us with three children and two grandchildren. All of our relationships are immensely enjoyed and precious to us, especially because we see them through the filter of God's heart, knowing that He is the Giver of these gifts we call family. "Every good and perfect gift is from above, coming down from the Father of the heavenly lights, who does not change like shifting shadows" (James 1:17).

Then there's Cassy! Our little add-on that we invited into our family several years ago. She has been, and continues to be, a constant source of joy in all of our lives. I never could have imagined that a 15-pound, scruffy, brown-eyed pup would add so much love to our family. Even when the inevitable, dark clouds of life hang overhead and completely obliterate the sun, Cassy is there, sitting quietly at our side in complete devotion to her masters. Just being in her presence often calms me down, which is not an easy task. Just ask my husband Joe.

The story of *The Little Prince and The Fox* was written in 1943 by the French writer Antoine de Saint-Exupery, and beautifully illustrates the special relationships many people have with their pets. The length of the story is too much for me to include in its entirety; therefore, I decided to share only some of its most poignant parts.

> "Who are you?" asked the little prince, and added, "You are very pretty to look at."

"I am a fox," the fox said.

"Come and play with me," proposed the little prince.

"I am so unhappy, I cannot play with you," the fox said. "I am not tamed."

"Ah! Please excuse me," said the little prince. "What does that mean— tame?"

"It is an act too often neglected," said the fox. "It means to establish ties."

"To establish ties?"

"Just that," said the fox. "To me, you are still nothing more than a little boy who is just like a hundred thousand other little boys. And I have no need of you. And you, on your part, have no need of me. To you, I am nothing more than a fox like a hundred thousand other foxes. But, if you tame me, then we shall need each other. To me, you will be unique in all the world. To you, I shall be unique in all the world ... If you tame me, it will be as if the sun came to shine on my life."

Aahh! I agree with the fox. This is truly a great story.

And this is exactly what happened with Cassy and me. She was just another dog among thousands, and I was just another human. Yet, when I began getting to know her while training her, and she began getting to know me, we bonded deeply. We became unique to each other, and came to need one other. And wonderfully, the sun did indeed shine on both of our lives.

However, as I think about her loyalty and devotion, I can't dismiss her *tame* countenance as it relates to GG, my granddaughter. GG was the first baby we welcomed into our family, and as far as I know, the only baby Cassy had ever been in the presence of.

When our daughter and son-in-law first ventured out with their precious new cargo, they placed the carrier which cradled their sleeping beauty carefully on the family room floor. All four of us gazed, gasped, ooh'ed and aah'ed at this little bundle of joy, anxiously waiting for her to awaken, so we could pick her up. In typical newborn style, GG slept for several hours with a look of blissful contentment occupying her angelic face.

After a few initial introductions to this new, very little human being, we were feeling a bit more comfortable leaving Cassy near the baby carrier. After all, I was not sure how this was going to go. Of course, I read up on bringing babies into the home occupied by a dog, but this was not any baby. This was GG!

As I recall, the four of us were somewhat apprehensive about how this debut encounter would unfold. How would Cassy react to the look and scent of a newborn? Would she show signs of jealousy? Would she accept GG into the fold? Would their relationship blossom into an enduring lifelong friendship or not?

We watched anxiously as Cassy fixed her gaze toward the baby. Her ears perked up, attentively. She slowly and cautiously took measured steps toward the carrier. Her stride was like that of a cat, as she meandered closer and closer to GG. As she approached the sleeping baby and slowly began to sniff her swaddled little body from head to toe, we all watched vigilantly, with bated breath, for any sign from Cassy that might indicate a problem.

Cassy then switched her gaze from the baby back toward us. Her previously perked ears were equally flopped over now, framing her composed, calm face. She circled the carrier, carefully looking for the perfect spot to plant herself. She let out a relaxed, audible breath before deciding to settle within inches of GG so she could provide protection and guardianship to her. What a relief! We all agreed that this relationship was off to a very good start.

Cassy was and continues to be gentle, sweet, and protective of GG, in addition to our newest little baby granddaughter, Gabby! Cassy immediately took her under her wing as well. Cassy will park herself near Gabby and quietly rest; however, when Danny, our son Michael's dog, came to visit, Cassy was on the alert.

There was no way Danny was going to get within three feet of the baby. Cassy transformed into a 15-pound infantryman ready to attack without hesitation. She began to utter low dull rumbling sounds and even exposed her teeth. I cannot believe I am putting this on paper; Cassy was aggressive! That's like a dove and a bloodthirsty hawk having lunch together. It just doesn't happen.

Anyway, because of her dedication to the family, Cassy drew the line in the sand with Danny (who just happens to be muscular and heavier than Cassy) and quickly took on the role of Alpha Dog. Cassy is a true companion; a loyal gal, and she most certainly lives up to the slogan as it relates to dogs, "Man's Best Friend."

"A friend loves at all times..." (Proverbs 17:17).

Jesus told his disciples in John 15:15, "I no longer call you servants, because a servant does not know his master's business. Instead, I have called you friends, for everything that I learned from my Father I have made known to you." Jesus knew these men intimately, and therefore, friendship with Him was possible due to the very personal relationship they had with Him. Jesus can and wants to be our protector and best friend also. He is a friend, who sticks closer than a brother (Proverbs 18:24).

Chapter 34: Will You Be My Friend?

Chapter 35

Wrapped in Safety

Several years ago, while working the night shift in the newborn nursery, it was imperative to wrap the newborns snugly in a blanket, like a Mexican burrito. This swaddling technique kept the baby feeling secure and minimized the normal involuntary Moro, or startle reflex, that all healthy newborns exhibit when they are suddenly disturbed or agitated. This firm, yet gentle, wrap provides just enough pressure to keep otherwise flailing arms snug at the baby's sides, close to their core.

Fortunately, most infants, when not swaddled with a blanket, are swaddled in the arms of their mother or father, sleeping peacefully. Most of us have seen (or heard) a baby who lacked a feeling of security. Typically, they will fling out their arms, tighten the body and let out a hair-curling wail accompanied by gulps of air and breath-holding. This physical response produces a scarlet red face, all of which add up to one unhappy neonate (along with frustrated parents).

Dogs, like babies, also need comfort during times of stress. Thunderstorms, fireworks and vet visits can be very unsettling for many dogs. Unlike newborns, dogs typically react to stressful situations by shaking, hiding in small dark places, pacing, or by putting their tails between their legs. A very popular and well-designed garment, known as The Thundershirt, is marketed toward dogs who suffer from anxiety and stress. The Thundershirt applies gentle constant pressure to an anxious dog in the same way a blanket is used to swaddle a baby. Apparently, as the garment makes contact with the dog's mid-section, he/she feels a circumference of force being exerted by the tight-fitting fabric. This, in turn, produces solace and reassurance.

When Cassy gets stressed, she has been known to lick her paws repeatedly, until they become sore and inflamed. She seems to be trying to soothe her anxiety with this repetitive obsession. Luckily, we have taught her to find comfort by retreating upstairs to the small windowless bathroom where she will typically sit in the dark away from the sights and sounds that gnaw at her peace.

Tucker, a sweet Bichon Frise belonging to my husband's brother Robert and his wife, Paula, chewed his tail raw one time because he was devastated by their absence while they vacationed. His love for his masters was so great, that he couldn't bear being separated from them, even though unknown to him, it was temporary. Thankfully, Tucker recuperated completely when Robert and Paula returned home, and life was back to normal.

Not all dogs respond to stress in the same way as Cassy and Tucker, much like people who don't all respond in the same way when life happens either. Is it possible to remain calm during the ups and downs of life? God tells us that it is. In John 14:27, Jesus Himself says, "Peace I leave with you; my peace I give you. I do not give to you as the world gives. Do not let your hearts be troubled and do not be afraid."

One unsettling event that I recall was when I was alone at my home just as an angry storm was brewing outside. The charcoal sky and damp air were clear indicators of the looming force preparing to interrupt the atmosphere. My husband was traveling and the only other living, breathing creature at home with me, was Cassy.

The forecast was not promising and broadcasters were suggesting that the sustained winds, although not of hurricane force, could do some serious damage. I wasn't worried. After all, I am a grown woman, and I had a loyal pet that would remain with me until the storm passed. Being the responsible person that I am, I was prepared, and knew I could handle this on my own. I had my smartphone, which doubled as a flashlight, bottled water, and candles—just in case.

I had decided that I would keep myself updated by tuning into the weather channel to better prepare for any unforeseen change in the course of the storm.

Just as I sank into my cozy recliner, remote in hand and my little scruffy girl on my lap, Poof! The power went out. No TV, no lights, and no sound, other than the intensifying rumbling noises I was now hearing from the gusty, howling winds in the distance. No worries, I thought. *At least, it's not raining very hard. We will be fine. I have Cassy and Cassy has me.*

Like a spark from a fire, my thoughts were immediately interrupted by a crash of thunder so loud that the windows in the room shook. Cassy took to the air as she sprung from my lap and bolted up the staircase to the small dark bathroom. There I was, sitting alone in the dark. My loyal companion had deserted me, and all I had, was a remote in one hand and cell phone in the other.

The sound of twisting branches and pelting rain was getting louder with each passing moment. As my heart began to race in my chest, I needed to gather my composure and do something; perhaps move to the center of the house, away from the potential shattering of glass from the windows.

As I moved to a safer area of my home, I called out to the Lord and asked for His protection. I recalled His promises to always be with me, even when I didn't necessarily like what was going on around me. "Be still and know that I am God" (Psalm 46:10). "God is our refuge and strength, an ever-present help in trouble" (Psalm 46:1). "Have mercy on me, my God, have mercy on me, for in you, I take refuge. I will take refuge in the shadow of your wings until the disaster has passed" (Psalm 57:1).

Eventually, the storm passed, and a welcome calm filled the previously agitated air. I could relax knowing that all was well and as usual, God had kept me, His child, safe even in the middle of a storm. Cassy quieted down as well, leaving her secluded retreat upstairs to join me in the living room, fully composed as if nothing had occurred.

As I ponder safety, security, and calmness, I am reminded of our very good friends, Bill and Jill, who live not far from us. They shared a story about their dog Chico that clearly exemplifies unwavering peace.

Several hours after a small snowstorm came through our area, Chico meandered outside. His owners, thinking he was just going to relieve himself and quickly come back inside after turning a patch of newly fallen white snow yellow, were surprised when Chico didn't immediately return. He instead parked himself on a mound of undisturbed powdery precipitation. The air was quiet, still and crisp, like a freshly picked autumn apple. He sat motionless, like a noble lion, content and without concern as he seemed to enjoy the calm after the storm.

Like the lyrics from a song by a well-known Christian artist, *Sometimes He calms the Storm and at other times, He calms His Child.*

God's word gives reassurance when we need it most, in the eye of life's storms. I will ground myself in Him and Him alone. Like Chico, I will rest, unmoved, no matter how unsettled life gets, in Him, knowing that He holds all things in the palm of His hand. Deuteronomy 32:10 beautifully illustrates how God tenderly cares for us, His precious loved ones. He keeps us as the apple of His eye.

Like a swaddled baby or an anxious dog comforted by The Thundershirt, He is there to wrap us in His protective love, peace, and safety, as long as we seek comfort in Him. The greatest security, so much more than safety during a storm, is the eternal security promised to those who place their faith in Jesus.

Salvation is found in no one else, "… for there is no other name under heaven given to mankind by which we must be saved" (Acts 4:12). Jesus Himself tells us in John 6:47, "Very truly I tell you, the one who believes has eternal life." The storms of life will pass; Thundershirts and swaddling blankets will be necessary no longer, but the word of God will last forever and ever. Now that's comforting!

About the Author

Carol Casale (a.k.a. CC) grew up in Brooklyn NY, graduated nursing school and married her childhood sweetheart, all before the age of 23.

Three children and several moves later, from New York to New Jersey to Connecticut to North Carolina (where she happily resides at the time of this book's publication) comprise the last 36 years of her life.

She enjoys cooking, entertaining, decorating her home and spending time with her family.

Never known to be an avid traveler or adventurer, bringing Cassy, her cherished lap dog into her life, just made sense. Little did she know this decision to become a dog mom would open up her eyes to the love relationship that prompted her to write this little book of tales.

CC's life motto is summed up by these words; Love The Lord, Love my family, Love my dog, Love life.

"CC" and Cassy